What We're Passionate About

An Anthology of Essays Written by America's Young Leaders and Activists

2017

Z Publishing Books

Edition 2017

Copyright © 2017 by Z Publishing, LLC

Published in the United States of America

Visit our website: www.zpublishinghouse.com

Table of Contents

About This Book

❖

The future can't wait for tomorrow.

Today's young people have grown up in a rapidly changing world, where political, social, and economic issues have reached the forefront of their collective consciousness. They eschew the option of sitting back and hoping for the best. Instead, they're taking the torch from those who came before them and lighting the way for future generations.

In *What We're Passionate About: An Anthology of Essays Written by America's Young Leaders and Activists,* more than 40 university students express themselves about the passions and causes that drive them. Whether devoting themselves to charitable causes or discussing their most cherished issues, these extraordinary young people prove that change can only come from within.

And while the problems of the world may seem overwhelming, there is no need to fear. With young people like these leading the way, others like them can be inspired to also become the change they want to see in the world. While every proactive action may not solve the issues that plague us, every young person who takes a stand *will* bring us that much closer. Because there truly are no lost causes – only lost opportunities.

"The future belongs to those who believe in the beauty of their dreams."

Eleanor Roosevelt

FeelGood
Mayank Mehta

An artist named Stephen wrote a song called *Sincerely*, and it's a call to action to those who love. It states: "There's a billion people that could use a hero. Come together, we're the tether of this love that's spinnin' around. We could be that miracle." These lines inspired me to re-evaluate my entire life and redirect the future of our collective story.

In fact, our lives are essentially roads full of short, vivid stories. I grew up on the roads of India—well, not literally, but let's say I did for the sake of the metaphor. What isn't a metaphor are the lives I saw while growing up there. You can see the worst of poverty alongside the best that money has to offer often on opposite sides of the same road. I've seen the suffering of kids who've literally grown up on the street on the same day that I've seen the privileged enjoy life's luxuries. My life is a story of living in between the unnecessary dichotomy, and it's a road of trying to resolve it.

The same is true for a lot of people. That's why so many humanitarian organizations exist. That's why so many people want to help. Maybe our actions stem from a desire to be a hero or to develop a strong sense of empathy or even a strong will to fight injustice, but they all lead to one thing: trying to help those in need. And, we've gotten better at it! We've become more creative, scientific, and strategic in our pursuit to save the world.

We've turned our emotional drives into a science. There are 5k runs, donation days, special events by massive corporations, galas, and so many other creative ways to donate to worthy causes. We're more strategic and business-like about it as well. For example, I'm part of an organization called FeelGood, and we've come up with a business model that allows us to make gourmet grilled cheese sandwiches for free. We get our ingredients via donations from generous companies, and this allows us to give our entire revenue to charity! An example of a logic-driven approach is the idea of being careful about the materials, and the amount of materials, we donate to countries in need. We've realized that uncurbed donations can actually hurt a struggling country's prospects for growth. As time has gone on, we've been figuring out how to save the world in countless numbers of ways.

All of this is heartwarming to hear, and we should congratulate ourselves on how far we've come, but we must keep in mind that we're not even close to done. Our stories are still in the midst of rising action. Stories of those who suffer are still as vivid as they ever were. Although we've become smarter, more creative, and more data-driven, we've overlooked one very important thing: collaboration. Right now, it feels like we're all on our different journeys loosely following a collective goal. We need to be more strategic. It feels good to say that we have 17 sustainable development goals we want to accomplish by 2030. What doesn't feel good is that we don't have a specific set of actionable items that we can split amongst ourselves and accomplish together. It's like we're functioning as five fingers instead of one fist. We've set a goal without a realistic, actionable plan to achieve it.

Now, more than ever, we need massive collaboration between philanthropic and humanitarian organizations to eradicate poverty. Now, more than ever, we need every person's efforts to be concentrated towards something greater. Grassroots efforts are wonderful, but we need to take extraordinary steps to fix extraordinary problems. Our loosely interconnected stories and efforts will help us save our communities, but it won't help us save the world. So we need to come together because we're the heroes and there are over a billion people who need us. We need to come together to be that miracle.

Under Your Wing
Gabriela Lozano Flores

I was born and raised in the Sultan of the North, commonly
known as Monterrey, Mexico, a crowded but picturesque city
encircled by mountains. Like any other big city, there is a
distinct division between wealthy and low-income
neighborhoods. I started to notice this at a young age. My
passion for helping those experiencing homelessness began
when I was a child. Being a restless and curious girl, I especially
started to observe children begging on the streets and how
desperately I wanted to learn more about their living
environments. "Why are they asking strangers for money?" I
would think to myself. It wasn't until I was older that I began to
understand the concept of homelessness and how this is a
global issue. To help the children, my mom and I would
donate non-perishable items and clothes to a children's
homeless shelter near my elementary school. As a child, I felt
accomplished but this was definitely not enough to satisfy my
restlessness to achieve more.

I moved to Iowa at the age of sixteen. Because of the
immense amount of opportunities given to students involving
academics, personal growth, and networking, I attended the
University of Iowa, the home of the Hawkeyes. However,
despite the abundance of opportunities, I noticed there was a
serious issue with homelessness in the Iowa City community. I
learned that Shelter House is the only non-profit organization

in Iowa City that is dedicated towards moving people in the community beyond homelessness. Although I did not know much about this organization, I looked up to their mission and what a few dedicated and passionate members envisioned our community to be—equity of opportunities and treatment for everyone. Under Your Wing was created after discussing with other dedicated, motivated, and passionate students about starting a student run organization associated with Shelter House in 2016. Under Your Wing is the first student organization at the University of Iowa to focus on helping Shelter House through volunteer work, fundraising for Shelter House needs, and uniting our voices to break stereotypes involving homelessness globally and in the Iowa City community.

There is a common misconception that those experiencing homelessness only involves individuals who make the streets their home and beg for money. While this may be true, there are many more instances where this is not the case. Homelessness may be experienced by someone who lost a family member, is a victim of domestic violence, a war veteran, a single parent, and many more contributing factors that people do not usually think about. One of Under Your Wing's goals is to raise awareness about this, since it is a subject not usually spoken about.

In the near future, Under Your Wing anticipates more members and volunteers in the Iowa City community to be knowledgeable and just as passionate as Under Your Wing members about the topic of homelessness and the equity of opportunities.

Undergraduate Advocacy for Human Rights
Maggie Brennan

❖

There is a point at which interest demands action. At this point, simply soaking in information fails to fill the void that forms upon viewing reality in motion. Keeping up with current news simply is not enough. This point is known as passion, and it drives my willingness to take any action to combat human rights violations, both domestic and international.

Every day we hear of human rights violations in our neighborhoods, on our campuses, in our country, and across the world. Similarly, every day we can soak in the history and evolution of violations in these same places. Knowledge and education of these actions molds the values we obtain as humans, but the passion I feel pushes me to communicate these violations to my peers, hopefully by educating my surroundings enough to make a significant difference to the course of human rights history.

At the University of Wisconsin (UW)-Madison, the Undergraduate Advocacy for Human Rights (UAHR) facilitates the passion shared by me and my peers. We are among a number of students who felt the need for an undergraduate presence that supports the work the existing Human Right Program at UW-Madison has been doing since 2013. This need echoes UW's already globally recognized brand, which makes a tremendous impact on a variety of research fields. As undergraduate students, we hope to positively contribute to this brand by implementing meaningful changes to human rights issues through raising social and cultural awareness of UW students on and off campus. In this perspective, we strongly believe that human rights advocacy is most effective when calls for reform are backed by a strong and informed public society.

In our country, the discourse of human rights is extensive, covering voting rights, indigenous rights, women's rights, rights to labor and education, as well as the failure of rights laws to capture the concerns many Americans face, such as members of a disaffected working class. These issues are deeply rooted in the institutions at the foundation of our country's existence. Within these institutions are ideologies and stereotypes that govern how marginalized Americans live day to day. These fundamentally problematic institutions result in human rights violations of the above mentioned groups, and it takes the efforts of those who educate others to influence change in these sectors.

Globally, universal human rights systems and international law focus on issues that threaten not only the US, but other countries as well. The current refugee and climate change crises are good examples of human rights violations. The right to a quality of life and a healthy environment are sectors where some populations are more privileged than others. In the cases of those who are not as privileged, human rights are violated. Again, it is through action that these will hopefully be addressed by policy changes here in the US and elsewhere.

Both domestically and internationally, mass populations are underprivileged because of the institutions that govern them. In these cases, human rights, rights that are believed to justifiably belong to every person, are violated. Learning about these violations is not enough; passion is imperative to drive action and yield change for the lives that need it the most.

Circle K
Taylor Majher

After receiving an inquiry about constructing an essay for this book, I immediately found myself planning out what and how I would write about my passion for the service organization I am a part of. The organization is Circle K, which is an extension of Kiwanis International. We focus on providing service to the Iowa City community, and I currently serve as the president of the organization. I have been a part of the Kiwanis family for seven years and have learned how impactful our service can be and how passionate I have become about this service. But, this organization is more than about the service and experiences I have accomplished. We are one entity, one group, made up of a diverse assembly of students that share the same strong desire to give back to the community. This proclamation is a collective work to express how each and every member shares the same passion for being a part of something bigger than themselves.

Kiwanis International is a global organization dedicated to supporting communities around the world, one child at a time, to ensure a successful future for those communities. The organization we are involved in is one of the daughter organizations of Kiwanis, which is on the collegiate level, Circle K. At the University of Iowa, we work with associations such as the Salvation Army, the American Cancer Society, and March for Babies. Our three main tenants are leadership, service, and fellowship and we stand by the motto: live to serve, love to serve.

To uphold these values, we volunteer at different events that many service organizations hold in the Iowa City community. We also create our own events for the residents of two houses located in the city, built and ran by the American Cancer Society. The Hope Lodge and the Ronald McDonald House are two partners within this society that provide a place to stay for many patients going through cancer treatment at the University of Iowa hospitals and clinics. The patients and their families stay there until their treatments are complete. They stay in large, comfortable rooms, have access to a kitchen to make all their own food, and have the opportunity to participate in any events that may be held by different groups throughout the week.

Circle K volunteers at the Hope Lodge every week and brings a different activity with each visit. Some things in the past have included a Bingo night, board game night, making crafts, painting pumpkins, and coloring. At the Ronald McDonald House, the residents always appreciate a good meal prepared by Circle K. We have made tacos, spaghetti, chili, and chicken noodle soup.

With each visit to the Hope Lodge, the people who receive our services are always extremely appreciative and want to know when we will return. The members of Circle K have also realized just how easy it is to brighten someone's day when they are going through a hard time in their life. Through these services, we have found that the smallest acts of kindness can make a huge impact on a person's life. When we play board games or simply color pages with the residents of the Hope Lodge, we are distracting them from the pain they may be experiencing from their treatment. We are taking those family members who are concerned about their loved ones in this situation away from those worries. We are talking with them, sharing with them what we are doing with our lives, and creating connections with them. We form meaningful relationships with them and giving them something to look forward to for the next time we visit. These activities are fun not only for the Circle K volunteers, but for the residents of the Hope Lodge as well; those two hours we are there with them brings them joy in their day. Simply talking with them and spending time with them has proven to be the greatest healing in this tough time in their lives. These small acts of kindness make a vast difference in their lives and we take that appreciation with us and implement it into our everyday lives.

We have become excited about service in all realms and to get even more involved with the other opportunities we have available through our organization, such as the Ronald McDonald House, where we spend two hours cooking a meal together and then serving it to those staying there. Through these services, we are able to connect with people who are struggling, who are in pain, who need some encouragement and motivation. We provide what they need by being in their presence and doing the simple tasks of cooking a meal and eating it with them.

Through just two of the many service opportunities we provide to the Iowa City community, we have gained a new perspective on what it means to be a volunteer. We have learned that this is more than a community filled with college students. We have learned that just being present, engaging with others, and forming relationships can make the largest impact of all. Most importantly, we have formed a new passion for service and have formed values that center around giving a little more than we take every single day.

Global Brigades
Sarah Murad

In the summer of 2015, I took a service trip to Peru to provide medical care to impoverished areas. The trip was coordinated such that the following services were provided to local people: dental care, medical education, medical exams, and pharmaceutical. One day, the group was on a bus travelling to the mobile clinic destination, when we came upon an 80-year-old woman living in a home made from trash. We decided to stop and check out the situation, when we found the elderly woman and immediately began providing medical assistance. During the examination, we discovered that her blood glucose level was above 500, (a glucose level above *300* is considered an emergency), and we rushed her to a nearby hospital. To my shock, when we arrived at the hospital, we found out that they did not have insulin, syringes, or anything to help her so she had to be transported to a hospital that was approximately two hours away.

Thankfully, despite the woman being in a serious condition, she received the medical treatment that was required and returned to her dwelling. We continued to monitor her diabetes and provide medical care for her other conditions. The group worked together as a team to build her a house and plant her a garden. Even though this woman had very nearly nothing (no family, no friends, no food, no income, no clean water, no toilet), she used what little resources she had to buy us each a pop/soda and greeted us with the biggest smile.

I was immensely moved by the positivity and generosity of the woman despite her deplorable living conditions and health. Before this trip, I did not understand the disparity people were living in and how heart-breaking poverty is, and the eye-opening experience put my cares into perspective.

When I returned to the United States, I realized that if I lent a helping hand to those in need and encouraged other people to join me, then we could work together through volunteerism to change lives and maybe change the world! I started a chapter of Global Brigades at George Washington University in an effort to instill a passion for volunteerism that would thrive even after I graduate. I want to make more people aware of how lucky we are to have clean drinking water, food, shelter, running toilets, access to education, access to medical care, or even medications. My goal is not only to bring awareness to global health and economic disparities but also to encourage people to do something about it. What will you do?

We're Better Than That
Hasan Nadeem

My grandmother was the strongest person in my life. Before she passed, she was the matriarch of a family comprised of doctors, scientists, and businesswomen that I simply call my mother, aunts, and cousins. My grandmother, or *Ammi*, boasted an open-mindedness that opposed traditionally conservative Pakistani culture. In fact, it was her opinion that settled a particularly contentious argument between my parents, eventually allowing me to invite girls over when I was in high school. Although it didn't happen all that often, it was the freedom to do so that helped me fit in better at school. As I look at all the women in my family today, I see my *Ammi*'s love, intellect, and grace resonate within them. The women in my family have taught me all I know about morality and it is undeniable that their views stem directly from the beliefs and character of my grandmother. The work I do, particularly as it relates to gender equality, is an extension of my *Ammi's* principles and is ultimately a testament to all the women who raised me.

My name is Hasan Nadeem, and I am the current president/co-founder of the group *We're Better Than That – Men Against Sexual Assault* at UW-Madison. My roommate had the idea to create the student organization after reading *The Macho Paradox*, by Jackson Katz, and proposed it to our group of friends. Instinctively, we knew that many men on campus believed in gender equality and figured the organization would occupy an unfilled niche in campus life.

We started our organization with a few goals in mind. First, we wanted to shift the burden of sexual assault prevention from women to men, so that more of the focus would be levied on preventing men from becoming potential predators. Secondly, we wanted to change the rhetoric regarding men's role in sexual assault so that it welcomed upstanding men to be more vocal about the issue. Finally, we wanted to create a space where men could candidly discuss issues like masculinity and gender inequality with others without feeling judged about a lack of knowledge or familiarity with the topics.

To push social norms in the direction of equality and inclusivity, our campus needed a call to men, from men. For too long, men were allowed to remain silent about the issues of sexual assault and gender-based violence. If we wanted to see a true change on campus, we needed the collaboration of organizations that sought to empower women and to diminish men's role as perpetrators. To accomplish the latter, we needed to have more honest conversations with the men on our campus. Only then, would we be able to develop a greater sense of empathy and compassion for the injustices that happen to women on a daily basis. Through understanding comes humility, and with humility, men can effectively support women to decrease cases of sexual assault. Without understanding the plight of women or much of the feminist work that has set the foundation of the women's rights movement as we know it, we will never truly be able to make necessary advances toward gender equality.

Our work not only addresses inequality between genders, but also permeates across various social issues. The institutions and systems that harbor determinants of gender-based violence are not dissimilar to those that perpetuate issues of racial inequality, economic shortcomings, and environmental instability, to name a few. Considering sexual assault as a stand-alone issue ignores the denigration and marginalization of many groups of individuals. The scope of our message is much broader and addresses several fundamental issues with society at the core. Ultimately, we promote the message of mutual love and respect for all human beings, regardless of creed, gender, or sexual orientation. Our group believes in a stance of altruism that can be cultivated within each and every individual through listening and understanding. It is this passion and belief that threads us together with a common focus and allows us to find happiness in the work we do.

I miss my *Ammi* dearly, and without her, I may have just been another boy who didn't feel comfortable standing up for the rights of women, or any individual's rights for that matter. Instead, I've found a true passion in fighting for equality. To me, passion is an outcome of the love and happiness that comes from work done in service to others. I am honored to work with so many people who share this viewpoint and have reinforced that women ought to be defined by their character, compassion, and intellect before their appearance. I find fulfillment in fighting for women's rights and though there is much work to be done, the people who have influenced me keep me resolute and optimistic about the future.

Continental Crossings
Ellyson Rae Martens

One of the selling points, for me, personally, in my decision to attend the College of Engineering at the University of Iowa was the introduction to the organization that I now find myself writing about: Continental Crossings.

I was deciding between Iowa and Purdue at the time. My father and I had driven from Chicago, Illinois to West Lafayette, Indiana, then on to Iowa City, Iowa, in a matter of twelve hours as a last ditch effort to compare the two engineering programs. Purdue had done a pretty good job of convincing me that their school was the one for me, and I didn't know if Iowa could compare. But, as I sat there in the Iowa Memorial Union, listening to various engineering students talk about the things they were involved in, the projects they were building, I found myself thinking less and less about comparing the two schools.

Then, Anthony, a civil engineering student, was asked to talk about the organization he was a part of: Continental Crossings. After Anthony had talked about Continental Crossings, Purdue was no longer even in the picture.

Continental Crossings has a very unique role in the College of Engineering at Iowa. It is part student organization and part civil engineering class. Our organization at Iowa is a branch of the organization, Bridges to Prosperity, whose CEO, Avery

Bang, is an Iowa alum. At Iowa, Continental Crossings raises funds, designs, and builds pedestrian footbridges in Nicaraguan communities that suffer from rural isolation. These communities are often times surrounded by rivers that flood for more than half the year, making it nearly impossible for community members to reach adequate medical centers, education, markets for crops, or job opportunities. During the summer, a group of six or seven Iowa students go down to a Nicaraguan community that is in need of our services and, in conjunction with the local people and Bridges to Prosperity, we construct our pedestrian footbridge.

There are many reasons why people get involved in our organization. Some see it as an excellent way to get relevant civil engineering experience, some use it as a study abroad experience, but everyone who participates in our organization has the same end goal in mind: to build something that will benefit a community in need.

I am so proud to be a part of this organization. Like so many of the students that are a part of Continental Crossings at Iowa, it sparked my interest on that college visit during my senior year of high school, and it remains a large part of my life years later. I will be on the travel team for the 2017 bridge, and I will be working alongside Anthony on his last project with us before he graduates, as well as five other travel team members and countless people back in Iowa who are invested in providing a quality product to well-deserving people.

Just the prospect of going abroad is exciting enough, but to add the element of helping to build something that will change people's lives for the better is not only more intriguing, it's empowering. As I work alongside the travel team members and students with new and innovative fundraising ideas, all looking forward to helping people they've never met, in a country they've never stepped foot in, it motivates me to view the world with a wider scope.

NAMI on Campus
Malaney Young

"I am inspired by the blinding brilliance of feeling that comes to me after a time of blankness. When the dulling fog lifts after a long depression, colors are more vibrant than I remembered them, smells are more intense, warmth is more penetrating. The hyper-awareness of all the wonders available to us, but invisible during depression, lasts a few days, maybe even a week. Then I slide into the delicious opportunity of taking good things for granted. During these times post-depression, I am struck by the rainbow of emotions available to me. What I take away is a promise to others on the other side of the fog that I will do whatever I can to support their journey toward wellness."

-Monica Akre, Founder

The National Alliance on Mental Illness is the nation's largest grassroots mental health organization dedicated to building better lives for the millions of Americans affected by mental illness. Founded in Fall 2016, our chapter aims to bring mental illness awareness and support to our community. The group is led by a team of five graduate students who aim to create a new set of resources that can help others prevail through their illnesses and succeed in their academic goals.

Approximately one in five adults in the US experience mental illness in any given year. Mental illness encompasses a wide variety of mental health conditions with a range of severity. Many people who identify prove to be resilient throughout their struggles, maintaining very successful and healthy lifestyles. However, sometimes these illnesses can be a source of deeper issues affecting relationships, health, and the safety of other people involved. Our group's mission is to provide services to those who are affected in any way by mental illness, to provide a stigma free and safe place for people to feel comfortable being and expressing themselves, and to let others know that they are supported and not alone. As graduate students, we believe it is important to maintain a voice for those in our community who live with mental illness. With graduate school being a mentally taxing place, fighting this battle to establish and maintain an equilibrium can provide further challenges.

NAMI on campus is an all-inclusive group, extending our resources throughout our entire community. We aim to eliminate the stigmas and discrimination that plague the lives of people living with mental health conditions. The negative stereotypes create just another obstacle in front of someone, making it harder to find peace of mind and comfort. We believe that with the proper support and acceptance, we as a community can overcome any of these barriers by helping each other to achieve the peace of mind and comfort that we all so very much deserve.

Chinmaya Mission Yuva Kendra
Sohan Phadke and Ruthvik Hejibu

❖

From a land far from the Americas, developed and refined over thousands of years, the Hindu culture has had a powerful impact around the world. This passage is a small excerpt about our passion for this beautiful culture. The adoration we bring here is shared between many of our peers and the youth of this very country, and we ask that you read with an open mind.

Our passion for Hindu culture is a product of what Hindu culture has done for us. As American born Indian students, we are fortunate enough to experience the strong familial ties between networks of people living half a world away. We have been bred with the kindness that comes from a group of people who give every object the respect it deserves, from a book, to a chair, to a teacher. Hindu religion, like most others, emphasizes the importance of family, especially of the parents. Without our parents, we are nothing, and the understanding of this is exemplified by the cultural norm where young adults do not leave their homes for college nor life beyond. The norm instead is to continue staying with one's parents throughout college, even through marriage and child-rearing years. It is a world view that is driven by familial love and creates homes where individuals routinely live with extended families. Each of our parents grew up in houses living with their cousins, uncles, and aunts, and have gifted us that familial love as well.

The second and perhaps more significant aspect that brings our passion for Hindu culture forward is the eternal respect given to all things. It is common practice in India, even after centuries, to prostrate to books or people that you have touched with your feet, as an apology for not giving them the respect they deserve. It is a culture where all beings are equal spirits, and when one adopts this world view, a certain clarity is reached. A doctor may be smarter than a janitor, but if either fail to do their job, the patient will suffer. If the doctor relaxes, the patient does not get the attention they deserve. If the janitor slacks off, the operating room is not clean and the patient contracts an infection. Understanding that all of us have a role to play, from the janitor keeping chalkboards clean for students, to the spider eating the pesky mosquitoes so that we can sleep peacefully, to the tree that provides cool shade on a summer day, reminds us of the vital importance and respect that everything around us deserves.

This culture we proudly call "our own" is one that is molded into each individual's perspective. This interpretation was only an idea of two college-aged students: wide-eyed, often labeled as naive, but completely enthralled by their culture's openness and acceptance. With this passage, we hope that you at least think about one of the unique cultures that live within America, a nation that so beautifully prides itself on being a melting pot. More so, we hope that our brief insight has helped give you an appreciation of the Hindu culture that we hold so dear.

The Wellbeing Committee
Anonymous

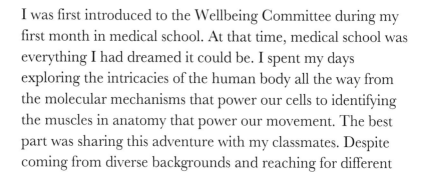

I was first introduced to the Wellbeing Committee during my first month in medical school. At that time, medical school was everything I had dreamed it could be. I spent my days exploring the intricacies of the human body all the way from the molecular mechanisms that power our cells to identifying the muscles in anatomy that power our movement. The best part was sharing this adventure with my classmates. Despite coming from diverse backgrounds and reaching for different goals, we all shared a common passion for bettering the world around us through the art of medicine. I felt supported by my family and professors to undertake this rewarding career and was excited for the path ahead.

Throughout my undergraduate years, I had relied on exercise, especially yoga, to center and strengthen my mind and body. When I got the email describing a medical school student group dedicated to student wellbeing, I thought it would be a great way to meet classmates that had similar interests in fitness. I came into the first meeting thinking I would just dip my toe into the group, but ended up taking the full plunge. I was put in charge of setting up a lunch lecture series for medical students on wellbeing practices. I was proud when my work for the Wellbeing Committee was recognized by the Office of Student Affairs when they offered me a summer internship to expand the committee. That summer, I fell off balance.

I had struggled with body image since high school, and would engage in behaviors like restrictive eating or over exercising that eventually stopped after a week. However, that summer, despite dedicating my time to learning about student wellbeing and taking a mindfulness-based stress reduction class, the unhealthy thoughts and behaviors grew until they eventually set up shop in my daily routine.

During my first year, many of my close friends in my class had opened up about their struggles with mental health. This brought me energy and purpose in my work for the Wellbeing Committee. I had hoped that some of the events I organized would be part of creating a culture that would be more conducive to addressing student mental health issues and that I could be a role model by contributing to a balanced medical school experience for them. Now, by some cosmic joke, I was simultaneously president of the Wellbeing Committee and deeply detached from my own wellbeing. I tried to hide my disorder from my friends and family, but they soon caught on. I was diagnosed with bulimia the winter of my second year.

Instead of shaming or retracting from me, as I had told myself they would, I was overwhelmed by the support I received from my classmates. I realized wellbeing is not a state, but a process. Wellbeing is not just a recommendation for us to push our patients, but also for us as future healthcare providers to encourage each other to incorporate this into our own lives.

Brands Give Back
Marissa Plescia

We are not just a fashion club, nor are we just an environmental club. We are an organization that aspires to combine the two—something that we think sets us apart from other clubs.

Brands Give Back is a club that promotes sustainability by hosting fashion shows with the hopes of raising money for The Rainforest Alliance, a non-profit organization that helps preserve forests, climate, wildlife, and more. Our goal is shown through our motto of "Fashion for the Forests," which proves our passion for fashion and the environment, a combination that is not often seen.

Our organization all began one year ago with our president, Emily Langtiw. Now a freshman at the University of Illinois, Urbana Champaign, she first started the club in her senior year of high school through which they raised $333 for The Rainforest Alliance. For this fashion show, they received sponsorships and donations from Gap and Banana Republic.

After her successful start, Emily continued Brands Give Back into college. She gathered an officer team of UIUC students, a group of people with varying talents and personalities, to help her achieve her goal. We have a group of members who help us plan the fashion show, raise funds, find sponsors and donations, and recruit more members. In April, 2017, we will host our very first fashion show on campus.

So far, our main goal has been to get our name out. We are now on Facebook and Instagram, and make regular posts about our organization. We have hosted several fundraisers with the help of local Champaign businesses like La Tea and Coldstone. We have also held a bake sale on our quad.

Our organization is one that we are greatly passionate about. With the environment being such a hot topic these days, we believe it is important find ways to improve it. But, we don't want to be just any environmental club. We want to intertwine it with our other passion: fashion. We believe that we can make a difference through these two facets: Stay sustainable. Stay stylish.

buildOn Community Team
Victor Lopez

I will never stop giving.

I have been thinking so much lately that people are so scared of kindness. They are surprised when someone shows love to others. In a world where we have gotten so used to hate, we refuse to believe that acts of kindness are truthful, and are nothing more but mere hypocrisy. I have chosen to take my passion to give to others to set a new goal for myself. That goal is to start a cycle of kindness, where people can trust one another and truly believe in each other.

My passion is based closely on those around me who showed me the beauty of giving their time for others, without ever expecting anything in return. While I was growing up, there was never a huge attention on community service until it was required by my high school to do it. It was at that point when I met students with a passion of their own that spoke volumes to me. They had committed their time to the homeless, to the elderly, to the children, and to those in need. For what? I wondered all the time why they continued to help even when they had surpassed their requirement for community service by over two hundred hours. But, sooner rather than later, I realized even without asking that they continued to help others because they themselves loved the feeling of meeting others and hearing their stories, seeing their smiles, and feeling their love and hope for other people being restored. That's when the importance of dedicating yourself to others over yourself came to me because it is that idea that truly brought me happiness.

The passion I have for service brought me happiness because I realized what I was truly giving to others. As I continued to connect with the children I spent two years with at an after-school program, I started to realize more and more that I saw the opportunity to give those children something I was never lucky enough to have: to have someone there to connect to, and grow with. Even if it was just to talk, or to help them with their homework, they truly felt thankful because of me being like a big brother to them all. It is the bonds I have made through service that have made me believe we can all truly love one another no matter what. We can give our time to others and find that one special reason to give. At this point, I wanted to live knowing I can make a difference, instead of pretending I was not there. I didn't want to live knowing that there are people who need help in the world, while I was just sitting idly by. I have embedded the hopes of the many great people I have met while volunteering, with hopes that as I continue, I can pass on that joy.

That is why I will never stop giving. I plan to give many more people my time. I hope to reach more and more people through service in hopes that I can pass on that kindness I received when my mentor, and good friend, gave his time for me. There is so much someone can find while helping others. They can find something they were missing, something they have been searching for or something new entirely. What is most important is that through service, bonds can be made in which you instill a cycle of kindness, and I hope to continue to help others in the hope that those people I reach will do the same for more and more people.

Just Breathe
Lindsey Knox

Becoming a veterinarian is not an easy process. It is burdened with countless hours of studying, exams, labs, and confusion. The sheer magnitude of commitment required by veterinary students leaves them with little time, energy, and psychological capacity they had before entering vet school. Unfortunately, this means personal hobbies and self-care are often left by the wayside. In all reality, the exact opposite should be happening, from the moment we walk through the doors to our last hours as practicing clinicians. Just Breathe formed with just that thought in mind and a passion to promote and explore health and wellness strategies that fit the hectic lifestyle of a vet student. We live by the motto of "you can't take care of your patients if you don't take care of yourself first."

As a struggling first year student, I looked around and thought my classmates had it all figured out based on the confidence they exuded so effortlessly. I hesitated to be the first one to admit that the burden felt too heavy until a friend said she felt the exact same way. There are others! Maybe there are classmates who, like me, are not sure of the exact way to approach a class/life balance successfully. In those first moments, we sparked the first conversations to normalize the struggles of a vet student by actually voicing them. Who would have thought that would work?! With this small act, a new passion for human connection with one another in veterinary medicine is becoming the new normal.

Slowly but surely, we are creating a culture of discussion and human connection with our colleagues on topics that have been historically difficult for vet students and even veterinarians to be open and willing to speak about. Fostering an environment of encouragement and comradery has grown that initial spark into a college-wide flame and led people to get out of their comfortable study bubbles into the real world outside of our campus. This has empowered students to take their wellbeing into their own hands, regain their self-help power, and know that there are support systems through this challenging experience.

Health and wellness is becoming more of a focus in veterinary medicine and Just Breathe has brought that to the UMN College of Veterinary Medicine. If just one person each year is reached and learns what self-care means for them, our student club is a success. With this insight into our club's passion and goals, I hope you have felt empowered to take a step back and reflect on what an important role self-care plays in your life. I want to leave you with wise words I have stumbled across in my search for wellness from Dr. Jim Nicolai as it perfectly captures Just Breathe's philosophy and can be applied to all aspects of life: "Where health is the destination, wellness is the journey."

Love Works
Marcus Miller

"But what's wrong with gender roles?" my friend, we'll call them Casey, asked me during one of our many long discussions about faith, theology, and the world. "God designed women to submit to the husband, just like God designed men to submit to the Church. We can be confident that since God says its good, then the fact that husbands have authority over wives is good."

Normally, I do my best to be open-minded and hear others' thoughts and perspectives. I am not so naïve to believe I have everything figured out—in fact, the more I learn the more I realize how little I actually know. However, I can't help but get upset about this conversation. Here we have Casey, who represents a large portion of "Bible-believing" Christians, using the Bible to justify harmful practices and attitudes—this time, it's sexism.

It's not just sexism, though. Throughout history, overt discriminatory behavior on the basis of race and racist attitudes was justified with writings from the Bible. The marginalization of LGBTQ folks continues to be perpetuated by many churches across this country.

While I do not go as far to say that every person who identifies as a Bible-believing Christian is misguided, I do believe that the institutions that reinforce the beliefs of such people are deeply rooted in a harmful way of thinking—that is, viewing the world as a black and white world, where people are either "Christian or not-Christian," "saved or unsaved," "in or out."

I used to be part of this culture. I attended a conservative Christian church for roughly five years and I was also very involved, even serving as an intern one summer. My official role was to assist in planning events for the youth group, as well as meeting with students one-on-one to develop relationships with them. At the time, I was fully invested in what I now call the mission of conservative Christianity. To be fair, some of the kindest folks can be found in these churches. While well-intentioned for the most part, I increasingly became uncomfortable with the self-righteous attitudes that pervade the culture, as well as the strict, narrow-minded view of the world.

The thing is, the "Bible-believing Christian" mindset comes with a set of beliefs that are unwavering: the Bible is the Word of God, the source of Truth comes from the Bible alone, belief in Jesus is the only way to Heaven—the list goes on and on. This encourages those attitudes that are extremely problematic. Beliefs about women being subordinate are OK—the Bible says so. Viewing LGBTQ people as inherently flawed solely because of their sexuality or gender identity is OK—the Bible says so. People who are not Christian are inferior and in need of converting, or they will suffer eternal suffering in Hell—the Bible says so.

So, while many of my duties as an intern were ostensibly to improve kids' lives, the ultimate goal was to bring them into the "in" crowd. To get them to become a Christian to avoid Hell. To be "saved." If the student already professed to being a Christian, then we wanted to make sure they adhered to a certain set of beliefs. Otherwise, it was questioned whether they truly were a part of the "in" group, and whether they truly were saved.

If someone truly is a Christian, they will certainly come to the same narrow understandings of the Bible as we do. This is the mindset that goes with the approach to faith that many churches take, and one that I used to be a part of for a while. However, after much reflection, I have abandoned this way of thinking.

The campus ministry that I started, Love Works, seeks to abandon all things rigid—dogmatic beliefs about the Bible are tossed aside. I guess the only thing rigid about us is the fact that we are unwavering in our support for the marginalized. We are unwavering in our support for full inclusion of LGBTQ individuals. We are unwavering in our commitment to loving our neighbors without the condition of trying to convert them.

We want to be a place where people feel no pressure to adhere to a rigid set of beliefs. Yes, you can be pro-life OR pro-choice here and not be ostracized. Yes, you can identify as non-religious and still be viewed as someone making an equal contribution to our discussions. Yes, you can openly state "Black Lives Matter" without being quieted by the disgruntled white folks who get anxious when conversations about race are brought up (in fact, we would probably join you in your fight for racial justice).

To make a long story short, we want to provide a space where everyone feels welcome to God's table. The reality is it's not my job to tell people who is "in" versus who is "out." This world is complex, with shades of grey coloring our lives. Here at Love Works, we believe in living life together without purporting we know the "right" answers.

While the Caseys of the world are certainly deserving of love and respect, the beliefs espoused by these people are harmful, as they draw lines, form boundaries and categorize people into little boxes. We don't find this helpful in connecting with God, others, or the world around us—which is what Love Works is all about.

Laughter Yoga Medicine
Susan Metzger and Benjamin Harbst

❖

Modern medicine is truly astounding. In a matter of decades, infections that use to be fatal are now cured with a pill. Mothers who, a century ago, would have died during childbirth now leave the hospital within a couple days of a routine surgery. As amazing as this progress is, us senior medical students have become acutely aware that the most effective medicine lies beyond pills and a scalpel. A human being has more sides than one, so why should his or her care focus on a single intervention?

We believe that modern medicine needs to incorporate a multi-modality approach to treat the whole individual. Exercise can be medicine, food can be medicine, laughter and love can be medicine. To that point, we believe that laughter in particular is an effective tool with untapped potential on the road to health. Laughter has been shown to decrease blood pressure, heart rate, and stress-hormones (cortisol, adrenaline) when experienced regularly. It has even been shown to have beneficial potential in notoriously difficult-to-treat chronic conditions such as migraine headaches and fibromyalgia. Laughter also boosts feel-good chemicals in the brain (endorphins), and reduces anxiety, in addition to many other mood benefits. The benefits don't stop there either—laughter has also been implicated in improving immune system's function through the newly discovered brain-immune system axis.

Many may be peripherally aware of this concept through popular media. The physician, Patch Adams, as popularized by Robin Williams in the eponymous film, introduced many of us to this thought. More recently, the Indian physician, Dr. Madan Kataria, has founded the practice of Laughter Yoga, which consists of practicing laughter exercises designed to induce forced or non-spontaneous laughter with peer groups. This inspired us to form our own group dedicated to laughter yoga within our medical school. We experienced first-hand the stress-relieving and energy boosting benefits of laughter yoga during our sessions among our colleagues. These sessions proved essentially valuable during times of intense communal stress, such as our final examinations. Laughter yoga is fun, free, fast, infectious, and can be performed anywhere, anytime, and with anyone. Whether attending organized group sessions or practicing with family and friends at home, laughing together for as little as ten minutes twice a week allows one to reap the health benefits. For these reasons, we feel we must voice our passion about laughter yoga as a potential therapeutic enhancement in the world of health care.

A medical chart does not capture the identity of an individual. A pill cannot be expected to relieve all of one's individual health concerns. Laughter is one more tool that can be used to treat the individual as a whole being. Doctors and patients work together in situations that often are the most disconcerting and anxiety-provoking times of the patient's life. During these times, doctors communicate with one another using complex medical language. Laughter, however, is a universal language. It can strengthen the bond between patient and doctor as they navigate the sometimes treacherous waters of physical, mental, and spiritual health. As Dr. Kataria once said, "There's not a lot of laughter in medicine, but there's a lot of medicine in laughter."

Tikkun Olam
Meghan Hill and Tatiana Lyons

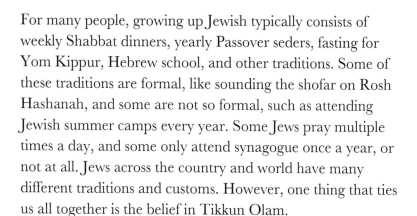

For many people, growing up Jewish typically consists of weekly Shabbat dinners, yearly Passover seders, fasting for Yom Kippur, Hebrew school, and other traditions. Some of these traditions are formal, like sounding the shofar on Rosh Hashanah, and some are not so formal, such as attending Jewish summer camps every year. Some Jews pray multiple times a day, and some only attend synagogue once a year, or not at all. Jews across the country and world have many different traditions and customs. However, one thing that ties us all together is the belief in Tikkun Olam.

Tikkun Olam is the belief that the world is fundamentally broken, and we as humans have a responsibility to consciously act to repair it. Repairing the world can come in many forms; for us, it means identifying and working to eliminate social injustices. This fundamental belief in repairing the world and caring for one another allows us to build community as for many of us, community is central to our Jewish identities. In our work, we are guided by the words of Rabbi Hillel (an influential Rabbi from ancient times), whose counsel instructs, "If I am not for myself, who will be for me? But if I am only for myself, who am I? If not now, when?"

As Jews, we are very familiar with the long history of oppression and prejudice our ancestors have faced, and even

43

now, anti-Semitism still exists in our society. This discrimination that is so deeply entangled in our identity has taught us to look out for each other. We know the dangerous power of silence and acquiescence, so we believe that collective solidarity with all communities is absolutely crucial to achieving justice for all.

When the rights of the LGBTQ community are threatened, we take action. When a corrupt criminal justice system is disproportionately affecting communities of color, we call our legislators to invest in people, not prisons. When our neighbors are not treated as equals because of their birth place, we march. When our communities face acts of homophobia, racism, transphobia, xenophobia, and any other form of hate, we stand with them in solidarity, just as they supported us in the midst of bomb threats targeting Jewish Community Centers. Not to mention, the Jewish community is completely heterogeneous. It is a dangerous misconception that all Jews are white. When Jews of color, LGBTQ Jews, and other Jews with intersecting identities are being erased from the narrative, we fight to center their voices. This is our responsibility as Jewish people. If we do not practice this activism and solidarity, we are abandoning Tikkun Olam, one of the fundamental tenets of Judaism. As the late Jewish Senator Paul Wellstone said, "We all do better when we all do better."

Tsidkatkha yiranenu: we are cheered by justice achieved, and sustained by the knowledge that the world forever turns toward the morning.

Empowerment
Andrea Poppinga

Over my course of almost a year and a half at Iowa State University, I have felt much empowerment and support from Iowa State University, not only as a female, but as a student in general. Iowa State has offered me so many tools and variations of support thus far. Every single day Iowa State University reminds me how lucky I am to be able to attend classes on such a beautiful campus, and have the same opportunities as all of my other classmates surrounding me. Life at Iowa State University is not dependent on your gender, but rather on your ability to put forth the effort and time to be as successful as you so choose.

I am motivated on a daily basis to do my very best in absolutely everything I do. Waking up at 7a.m. every morning for my 8a.m. classes is not always easy, but I am reminded of what will come of it in the future. I am motivated by being the most successful woman I can be in my field of work. I want to break stereotypes, and I want to end the thought processes of those who think women cannot be as hardworking or as smart as men. It simply is not true, and unfair to women who work day in and day out to provide for their families, while never receiving the recognition they deserve.

Empowerment is all about planting the seed to share your knowledge with someone else, and choosing to inspire those around you on a daily basis to be a better individual. I think every individual has the opportunity to empower those around them each and every day. I provide empowerment to those around me by positively motivating them to not only be better in school, but also be a better person all around. Don't get me wrong, going to class, getting assignments and projects done in advance, and always choosing to participate in classes are definitely important ways I choose to empower people, but what about the more important life-long ways of empowering those around you? Letting others know how special they are, how much value their life, adds to yours, and how having great character is one of the most important things you can have in life; those are the bigger picture things I choose to bestow in others and empower individuals around me with on a daily basis.

This week is all about women empowerment and how important women are to our society. Although I think it is extremely important to recognize women and all they have done throughout history and modern day to create meaningful change, I think this week should be focused on both men and women and positive changes to our society as a whole. We can be tools of support to one another every single day. It is important to stop minimizing the hard work and the talent of one another, based on gender, and start recognizing and supporting one another to make this world a better place for the short time we have here on Earth.

Water Environmental Federation
Grant Balkema

Everyone is aware that we could not survive for more than a few days without water. Yet, so many of us don't seem to care about polluting this vital resource. The state of the bodies of water we use are a clear example of Garret Harden's *Tragedy of the Commons*. Environmental sustainability, particularly as it relates to water, has been a long-standing interest of mine as a junior at the University of Illinois in Urbana Champaign. As co-president of the Water Environmental Federation (WEF) UIUC Student Chapter, I have spent countless hours reviewing water quality issues. My passion for water, however, extends beyond my college experience.

I spent years competitively rowing on the Charles River and teaching kids to sail on the Boston Harbor, where the Charles River empties. The Charles River used to be one of the most polluted urban rivers in the nation, emptying into an even more polluted harbor. It smelled horrendous, looked dirty, and was unsafe for boating, let alone swimming. Over time, through the diligent work of civil engineers and aquatic scientists, the Charles River has now become one of the cleanest urban rivers in the nation. Without this work, I would never have been able to row on the Charles River, an experience deeply ingrained in my identity. This is a large reason why I have a deep appreciation for the aquatic environment and feel that I have a duty to give back to it. WEF is full of dedicated environmental engineers who have a similar passion to keep our waterways clean.

The WEF design team competes to solve a real-life problem in the water industry. This year, the topic was to design a wastewater collection system and treatment plant for a town in Costa Rica. This town currently uses septic tanks that are frequently emptied straight into the ocean. Our goal was to solve this problem. The WEF design team is a great opportunity for students to work on a real-life application to their studies and apply their knowledge to something they truly care about, such as the Costa Rica wastewater problem. This competition is a great way to give back to the community and to showcase to everyone that we all have a responsibility to maintain the quality of our water around us.

WEF is full of passionate students who want protect aquatic environments for numerous reasons. This past summer, I interned at the local Charles River Watershed Association (CRWA) near my home in Newton, MA. I conducted a substantial amount of *E. coli* and *Cyanobacteria* monitoring throughout the Charles River along with fieldwork for other surrounding tributaries in the watershed. In addition to my internship, I worked part time at my old job as a sailing instructor on the Boston Harbor. I noticed this summer that the water was discolored in the locks where the Charles River and the Boston Harbor meet on my way to the Navy Yard one day. The next day, I tested the water for *Cyanobacteria* using the training and equipment from my internship. I did this on my own time and discovered that there was, in fact, *Cyanobacteria* in the locks. After reporting my findings to the EPA, I heard about it on the news a few weeks later. This real-life experience expresses my dedication and passion for my work with water sustainability, and exemplifies the sensitivity of our aquatic surroundings. This passion towards our work is the essence of the WEF-AWWA UIUC Student Chapter and all our students are willing to do the same to protect what we love.

Native America
Sydney Paysheninne

❖

A view of our world through an Anishinaabe Kwe's perspective:

Every being has a purpose on Turtle Island.

Our Creator made sure the Anishinaabe people had everything that was needed to survive. Prior to colonization, we, the two legged beings, understood our responsibilities to Mother Earth.

We are physical beings in a spiritual reality, and our language (Anishinaabemowin) continuously represents that aspect of walking through our lives. Anishinaabemowin gives life to objects typically considered inanimate in the English language. Paired with traditional teachings, this gives Anishinaabe people an understanding of our duty as two-legged beings under Father Sky, upon Mother Earth, Nbiish (water), the winged beings, the four-legged beings, as well as our own brothers and sisters. What our ancestors before us had done to ensure we have a way to live continues in a cycle we must sustain for generations to come after us.

Turtle Island was created and indigenous people lived here in our traditional ways prior to colonization. Anishinaabe people were on familiar land in a place the Creator (God) had intended for Anishinaabe people. Turtle Island was familiar and recognizable to our people, and there we had established our lives.

Mni Wiconi: water is life (Lakota language). Nbiish bmaadziwin aawan: water is life (Anishinaabemowin language).

There is no alternative to water. Water, or Nbiish, is the source of life for every being on Mother Earth. Let me explain what I mean by "being". All beings, or all things, on Mother Earth have a spirit and are alive. Therefore, every being on Mother Earth needs water to survive. As Anishinaabe people, it is our duty to protect our Mother and all her sources of water.

Most importantly, it is crucial to remember that, yes, environmental activism is in place to protect current generations, but indigenous people strive to protect *all* beings. This is especially emphasized for generations to come after us. Traditional teachings show us the importance to conserve, protect, and to sustain.

Every being on planet earth is composed of mainly the same elements. Yes, every being on Mother Earth is different, but when the compositions are broken down, they are all nearly the same. Most things on earth are composed of water—overall, the human body is 70% water. The only thing that is different is our purpose and how we appear in physical form.

For anybody reading this right now, this is not nearly enough of an introduction into the depth of our indigenous culture. If you arc unfamiliar with the culture, you will probably never understand the way it works. Walking through life is a process I will continue to learn until the day I walk on and leave the physical world. I will end with this, however. The fact that I know so very few people that I am protecting speaks louder than anything I could ever say myself. I cannot take credit for the things I have done. For one, because I am not accomplishing anything alone, secondly because teachings I have learned have shown me I am part of the world's ecosystem. Beings who cannot speak or appear visible to the naked eye share the same amount of importance in this ecosystem as I do. I am worth the same as every human being on earth, and the world holds my brothers and sisters. This is why I do what I do. For all human beings, and for all generations.

I am Waabishkaa AsiniiKwe and I have spoken. Miigwech.

National Society of Black Engineers
Greg Brooks JR

My name is Greg Brooks. I am the president for the Youngstown State chapter of the National Society of Black Engineers (NSBE). I was also a counselor for my school's Summer Bridge program. Both NSBE and Summer Bridge have helped teach me to be a leader. I have learned that you do not have to always be heard to be a leader. Many true leaders let their actions speak for them and they make things happen instead of talking about them. A quiet leader can be just as effective as a leader who is always trying to get their view across. Summer Bridge is a program that helps minority students transition from high school to college. It helps prepare them and shows them how college works and is setup. We guide them through campus and show them around the university and explain what it is like. That program made me a better person because I enjoy helping people, especially those who possibly look up to me. I enjoy making a difference and helping other students when I can. NSBE is an organization that helps minority students, who are usually African American, to network with businesses so they can gain networking and professional skills. Ultimately, the goal of NSBE is to help these students gain internships, co-ops, and eventually full-time jobs with these companies. NSBE has contributed to my education a lot. It is one of the major reasons why engineering is still my major and why I am still at YSU. It has motivated me in the classroom by exposing me to all the opportunities open to me in my future if I continue to work hard. It has made me a better person because this opportunity has made me more open minded and accepting of change and new things. I have become a more well-rounded man because of this experience.

Deliberate Connections
Amy Olejniczak

❖

I am passionate about creating and sending meaningful messages.

The handwritten letter is an important and enduring feature of our world's history. Persian Queen Atossa composed the first recorded handwritten letter circa 500 BC. The stamped letter we recognize today emerged during the reign of Queen Victoria in 1840. The United States introduced a limited postal service in 1842 and standardized stamps in 1847.

In an increasingly digitized society, illuminated screens and instantaneous messages characterize modern connections. In spite of the beneficial uses of technology, there is a notable disconnection between the written word and what we type on our screens. Although we are communicating more, we appear to be saying *less*.

A handwritten note is intentional, indelible. It requires time and thought to write messages that matter.

Hannah Brencher, founder of the global non-profit, The World Needs More Love Letters, explains, "Even though love covers all things, fear is what keeps us silent and keeps words unsaid. Fear keeps us standing in one place. Eventually, when it wins, it means we never got the courage to say what we needed to say." Thoughtful composition ensures we have the opportunity to say what we believe, say what is necessary, and

55

say what is just in a bold, permanent way. The World Needs More Love Letters and Campus Cursive chapters all over the world aim to spread kindness and encouragement through handwritten letters to strangers.

All it takes is a few words to let someone know that you care about them, you are grateful for them, and you believe in them. Handwritten letters not only uphold time-honored traditions, but are also a small way to create a lasting impact.

Letters are permanent, unchanging. To foster a community that values words and cultivates consideration, we must engage in deliberate actions. Handwritten letters are an opportunity to reflect on the world around us, share our stories, show empathy, and inspire a generation.

What Lies Ahead
Camille Mero

I grew up in the elite sporting environment of Olympic level figure skating, exposed to athletes enduring the daily rigors of physical and mental exhaustion. I watched as they suffered disappointment in their careers yet always found the will to get up and try again. They excelled at every angle of their life even if they failed at it the first time. As a young girl, my parents did me the greatest favor by taking me to the ice rink at age four in the morning to watch these athletes work. Once I was old enough to skate, I was able to partake in their training beside my mother and father as their coaches. I'd skate around the edge of the rink to monitor that the skaters were staying a legal distance from the borders. I'd perform in any stunts just for the chance to be thrown in the air. But, most of all, when a skater fell down, I would hustle over to their side to help them back up as my parents guided them on how to conquer their stunt. Needless to say, they never ceased to try again and, even if it took a hundred times, perfected that jump then went on to learn a new one. By being exposed to perseverance at a young age, I quickly learned that if I want to accomplish anything in my life I would be proud of, quitting is never an option.

Endurance is a trait that was instilled in me at a young age and has continued play a leading role when faced with, what felt like, impossible obstacles. The goals I have are not ones that are going to be accomplished easily and there have been times where all odds were stacked against me, but when I hold the memories I created during my time on the ice, I have confidence that I will overcome anything because I don't know how to give up.

When posed with the prompt to write about what I'm passionate about, I choose to focus on the chunk of my life where I was gifted with the opportunity to learn that even when life doesn't go as planned, there is always a way to accomplish your goals. I am passionate about the challenges I am faced with every day. I feed off the will power to surmount everything thrown my way. My passion for challenges is the driving force for why I want to peruse a career in Pediatric Oncology and why I find A Moment of Magic to be such an inspiring organization. When children are diagnosed with cancer, they have to find the power to take on their own challenge at such a young age and as a Pediatric Oncologist, I'd be able to help guide them in order to do so. Because this goal is long term, being a part of A Moment of Magic is my next goal in making a difference in these children's lives to help them overcome their challenges and watch them grow into wonderful people. A Moment of Magic instill the values of being brave, strong, and fearless into their members and the children they visit. Their core values are essential in taking down challenges and are characteristics needed for all people in order do the impossible, whatever that may be to them.

Addiction Advocacy
Kelsey Hennig

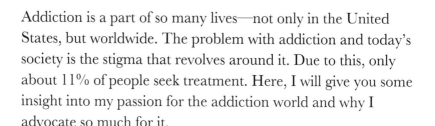

Addiction is a part of so many lives—not only in the United States, but worldwide. The problem with addiction and today's society is the stigma that revolves around it. Due to this, only about 11% of people seek treatment. Here, I will give you some insight into my passion for the addiction world and why I advocate so much for it.

My passion for addiction comes from a place of caring and concern for what our society has become. From my own family experience, I learned early on the effect addiction can have on one's family and friends. This is where my desire first stemmed from; my goal was to become more knowledgeable and understanding about this other world that so many people end up in. I felt as though many people were misunderstood and were not given the hope and encouragement they needed to get through something dark that was taking over their lives. By being a student of the Alcohol and Drug Studies program, I was able to take that first step in raising awareness on this topic.

Advocating for this cause was my number one priority when I decided to major in Addiction Studies. Without advocating for what you are passionate about, how can you expect to see a change happen? This is where our student organization, the Coalition of Addiction Students and Professionals Pursuing Advocacy (CASPPA), comes into play.

As a part of the organization, we take our passion and drive to help those in not only the community, but also the state of South Dakota as a whole. We advocate in ways such as going to Washington D.C. for Hill Day, where we speak with our state legislators about the bills we would like to see passed in order to help the addiction profession. This is a big step in helping spread awareness within the state of South Dakota, and the world as a whole.

Addiction is complex and often avoided. When discussed without the passion of individuals in recovery or those that suffer from familial ties, it does not get the attention in needs. Though I am only one student, I know I can make a difference and I plan on doing so for the good of others. With this passage I have written today, I hope it can bring more awareness to the world of addiction to inspire others to want to help be a part of the solution in ending the stigma. It's not always an easy disease to understand, but those suffering can't go through it alone.

Why Diapers Matter
Morgan Clark

When I tell people I'm passionate about diapers, I often get blank stares. "Oh, okay," they respond with empty nods. It doesn't take long for me to jump into my spiel and begin explaining why they mean so much to me. Most people are kind enough to indulge me for a few minutes, but after hearing just a little bit about what I'm doing, they usually stick around to hear me out.

When I was in my senior year of high school, I volunteered in the nursery at a local hospital. I was stocking the patient rooms with linen one day when I overheard a conversation between a new mother and a nurse. The mother was asking where she could find diapers for her baby. They were expensive, and she just didn't have the means to pay for them. To my surprise, the nurse didn't have an answer for her. They could provide a pack or two to send home, but after that, she was on her own.

When I returned home after volunteering that day, my curiosity got the better of me and I started to Google. I was surprised that 'diaper need' was a popular search. Thousands of things showed up, and the first article I clicked on was a study about diaper need from the Yale School of Medicine. They cited that mothers who struggle to afford diapers for their children are far more likely to experience postpartum depression.

As I continued reading, I found out that one in every three moms in the United States reports struggling with diaper need. This inability to provide such a basic need for her child is what contributes to postpartum depression, and makes it even harder for her to care for her child. An adequate supply of diapers can cost about $900/year, which amounts to a woman working full time at minimum wage and spending almost 6% of her gross income on diapers alone. Additionally, federal aid programs such as WIC and SNAP don't cover diapers.

Another compounding issue is that day care centers typically require diapers to be supplied with the child. This means that a lack of diapers keeps children out of early childhood education, and mothers out of work.

This issue spoke to me because it was so much more complex than it appeared on the surface. Finding a way to provide diapers to families in need seemed like a tangible way to contribute to their lives. A clean diaper means a clean baby. Clean babies are happier and healthier. And, when mothers can go back to work, they will eventually be able to afford the diapers they needed so badly to begin with. I founded Make A Change to do exactly that—start making a change in the lives of the women and children in my community through diapers. We're a group of students who care deeply about contributing to others, and we've found a really good way to do that. Spreading the word about diaper need and holding diaper drives has become one of the most impactful parts of my college career, and I can't wait to see it continue on after I have graduated.

Feeding Others, Fulfilling Ourselves
Reed Trende and Drake Krohn

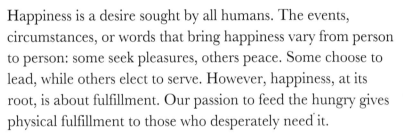

Happiness is a desire sought by all humans. The events, circumstances, or words that bring happiness vary from person to person: some seek pleasures, others peace. Some choose to lead, while others elect to serve. However, happiness, at its root, is about fulfillment. Our passion to feed the hungry gives physical fulfillment to those who desperately need it.

Our passion is more than lending a helping hand. We understand the dire need for nourishment. Without food, it is difficult to focus and function. As Maslow's Hierarchy of Needs addresses, when a person's psychological needs are not met, they are motivated to look for food above all else. When people are famished, safety, social acceptance, and self-esteem are abandoned. Without food, the base of Maslow's pyramid is missing, and there is no way to advance to higher levels of fulfillment. This basic necessity in life, something many of us take for granted, is the utmost priority for over one billion people who go without food every day.

Now, feeding over 13% of the world's population who are hungry seems impossible. Nevertheless, this challenge only fuels our passion to serve. Hunger, like any global issue, is not solved overnight or even in a lifetime. However, with thousands of people's help, positive improvement can and will be achieved.

Organizations like the World Food Programme, Feed My Starving Children, and Land of a Thousand Hills can all provide several meals to those in need for as little as a dollar. This relatively small contribution of a few meals has an extensive impact for those who are fed. These small contributions have helped to reduce worldwide hunger by 23.4% since 1990[1]. This progress offers encouragement for the fight against hunger, as well as a positive outlook for the continued decrease in world hunger in the future.

In the fight against hunger, another passion of ours is to serve. The organizations listed above, in addition to thousands of others, offer various volunteering opportunities. Ranging from sorting and serving food to fundraising and financial operations, each experience is educational and enriching. Therefore, helping at these organizations does not feel like a task, but is genuinely a humbling and enjoyable experience. Though all non-profit volunteering experiences have a sense of doing good work for the community, there is something special about food organizations. Feeding the hungry is such a strong testament to the fact that several people doing small things for others can have a tangible and visible impact. To feed others and help to eliminate a daily source of their concern is complete fulfillment for us.

Ultimately, there are an infinite number of positive actions that people can do for one another. Feeding the hungry just happens to be a passion our heart called us to do. Now more than ever, technology has made it easier to connect those who can help and those who are in need. Additionally, a physical gain for one person can be a spiritual gain for another person. As is stated in Philippians chapter two, verse four: "Let each of

---

[1] worldhunger.org

you look not only to his own interests, but also to the interests of others" (English Standard Version). There is nothing greater you can do for someone than to serve them. We hope our words have opened at least one reader's mind to food insecurity and world hunger, and encourage everyone to find a local food organization and try volunteering. Trust us, it will be well worth it.

Vegan Voices
Arianna Barley

I'm going to make one generalization about humanity.

We all love the planet we live on, and we're all interested in the diversity of live that inhabits it. It's a part of human nature. Our compassion and our never-ending curiosity in the complexities of the world we inhabit propels us forward and sets us apart from other species. I have grown to deeply admire this about humanity, and as I get older and more aware of the intricacies of the world, I feel that it is my duty as an inhabitant of earth to learn as much as I can in addition to doing my part to maintain its beauty and longevity.

However, taking a close look at the systems that we as humans have put in place can seem a bit counterintuitive to human nature. I hadn't really explored this idea or how the actions I was taking every day were contradicting what I truly cared about until freshman year of college. Like so many of us, I watched a documentary on Netflix that left me feeling unsettled and confused. But for me, it didn't stop there.

This documentary, "Earthlings," revealed the true, unfiltered nature of meat and dairy production. There were no images of a happy cow in a field of daisies, but rather, hundreds of cows packed tightly together in a factory as their calves are taken from them and used for veal, and images of animals being slaughtered in ways that were less than humane or sanitary. Hardly the images you want to accompany your hamburger and milkshake.

I decided to look a little further into the meat and dairy industry and do more research, and I found that they are also one of the leading contributors to global warming. I delved further into the overwhelming statistics against the meat and dairy industry, and, the more I learned, the less appealing the food produced by those industries became. It really all boiled down to the fact that what aligned with all the things I was truly passionate about—peace, love, humanity, and nature—was veganism. My values were being contradicted by my decision to consume and, therefore, support those industries, and that didn't sit well with me, so I decided to put my money where my mouth is and adopt a fully vegan lifestyle.

I find being a conscious consumer to be one of the most important and influential actions in today's world. I believe that our one true voice in our fast-paced, money-driven society is our vote. In political elections, sure. But, I'm more concerned with how we use our voices on a daily basis through our actions. In this respect, being vegan for me is about using the one voice I have and doing my best to support the industries that I believe in. The fact of the matter is that the meat and dairy industries work against the environment I love exploring, the animals I love protecting, and the peace I love promoting. By choosing to be vegan, vegetarian, or even just consume less meat and dairy on a regular basis, we are communicating to these industries that there should be less demand and production of these harmful products.

For me, living as a vegan is my way of leaving a positive mark on the world I love. I want to know that I at least did what I could with the life I was given to positively impact the

67

world that I love living in. I want my children and my grandchildren to able to say that I was one of the people who took small steps to make their living conditions better. I am passionate about veganism because it makes me feel so much closer to the earth and the animals I love and it makes me think more than I ever did before about the industries I choose to support.

I have been vegan for almost three years now and it has opened my eyes to a wide spectrum of issues concerning environmental, human, and animal rights. It is a lifestyle that compels me to learn more every day and be conscious of the mark I leave on the world. I continue to learn more every day and I plan on always doing what I can for the betterment of humanity and the planet.

We Are People First
Jamaica Cooper

In high school, I had a pretty difficult time accepting the adversity that comes with having a disability. Now, I am grateful for what I have learned by having a disability. This essay is about how I've used my disability, the thing that I thought I would never come to terms with, to help others.

Life can be difficult for anyone, but I believe that life can sometimes is even more difficult for those with disabilities. In the midst of life's pre-existing challenges, people with disabilities often face their own incomparable and sometimes unrecognizable challenges. Though we as a society are becoming more and more inclusive, we still have a long way to go. I use my gift of advocating for those with disabilities to help raise awareness about our abilities rather than our disabilities. My goal as an advocate has never been to teach people why equal opportunities matter, but to be an example so others can see firsthand why it is so important.

I think an important factor in truly accepting differences is to get comfortable with differences. My passion lies in embracing and 'normalizing' differences, and that effectively starts with knowledge that being different is okay.

Once we as society get comfortable with differences, our minds are open and more accepting of the uniqueness in the world—different isn't less.

I think an important aspect, and perhaps the most important aspect, to take away from this is that we (people with disabilities) are people first! We have passions and dreams just like everyone else in the world. We want to be seen as a person rather than a disabled person, but more importantly, I hope I have shed or added some positive light on your perspective of people with disabilities. Equal opportunities matter.

Students Enhancing Resources for Vermillion Enrichment
Christian Pollema

❖

Vermillion, South Dakota, is a small, charming college town tucked away in the southeast corner of the state. This community boasts a population of approximately 10,700 people, making it the eleventh largest city in South Dakota. Home to the University of South Dakota (USD), a large component of Vermillion's populace consists of college students, though the town is also home to many other demographics. In efforts to become more involved in enriching the community around them, students at USD have taken it upon themselves to develop and sustain the organization, Students Enhancing Resources for Vermillion Enrichment (SERVE).

This organization is composed of seven branches, each targeting a different demographic or social group within Vermillion. They are as follows: Adopt-A-Grandparent, Big Pal Little Pal, Bridges, Cultural Connections, Adopt-A-School, Heroes, and Variations in Volunteering. Each branch requires a commitment of one hour a week minimum, in which participating college students spend time with or help a member of the surrounding community. Adopt-A-Grandparent helps the elderly, while Big Pal Little Pal, Adopt-A-School, and Heroes reach children ranging from 5-14 years old. Members working with Bridges spend time with cognitively disabled individuals, those with Cultural Connections are partnered with international students, and Variations in Volunteering connects participants with different projects and businesses in Vermillion.

SERVE is an organization that prides itself on the mutual benefits it delivers for its members and those they help. First and foremost, our mission is to serve Vermillion in a variety of ways to ensure it is an optimal community for all its citizens. By offering its members opportunities for service-based learning, SERVE simultaneously aims to develop engaged students who understand the importance of active citizenship within their communities and have a passion for the people that inhabit them. It is too common for students to become so engrossed in activities within their universities that their scopes do not span beyond their college campuses. It is our hope that by cultivating positive volunteering experiences off campus, we simultaneously cultivate life-long attitudes toward learning by interacting with and serving their surrounding communities.

A Universal Bond
Christopher James Santos

In today's society, people often become consumed with
material goods and possessions, yet when I traveled across the
world, I met people who lived with limited resources, however
what little they did have they shared with those around them.
Thousands of miles away from America is a small village called
Chintsa, South Africa, were people who have very little, look
out for each other and are constantly happy. This passage is
about my experience in this small village and why I was
inspired to start an organization to help the kids of Chintsa,
South Africa.

My passion to help the kids in Chintsa originates from a
four-week volunteer trip with International Student Volunteers.
While volunteering I came across two very different lifestyles:
that of the town of Chintsa and that of the township, also
known as "Location 16". The town consists mainly of beautiful
mansions on the ocean while the township, which is less than a
five minute walk away, is made up of 300-400 metal huts.
While in the township, I met a man, who had found spare gym
equipment and construction material and was able to build a
gym in the community. However, rather than charge people to
use the gym, this man opened up the gym to everyone in the
village for free. The reason he did this was because the village
of Chintsa embodies an African ideology and mindset called
Ubuntu, which means, "Human-ness". Ubuntu is a Universal

bond that connects all of humanity. The idea is that if one person has, we should all have. I realized that this was the ideology of all the people in the township, and was a mindset these children grew up practicing.

One day, while on a lunch break, this concept was further exemplified. After eating my lunch, I realized I had some extra pizza and decided to give it to a young child. Immediately, when I gave him the pizza he started to run home. I was extremely confused at why the little boy would do this. I was later told that he went home to share the pizza with his family because he also embodied the principal of Ubuntu and would not eat without sharing with his family.

When playing with local children towards the end of my trip, I too realized that I wanted to embody the philosophy of Ubuntu. In Chintsa, all of the people in the village look out for the children so kids are able to wander freely. One of the kids I ended up playing with eventually signaled that he wanted a piggy back ride. After some time of carrying this boy on my shoulders, I looked down at his bare feet. To my astonishment, his feet were cut up and bloody—his toes seemed to be webbed and mutilated. The boy's feet ultimately suffered constant irritation since he did not own shoes. It was at this moment I realized that I could not go home to multiple pairs of shoes and leave this boy with nothing. I realized I too needed to embody the concept of Ubuntu and start a club to fundraise for kids who didn't have basic necessities, since I had so much. I named the club, Helping Chintsa, since our focus and only goal is to help the kids of Chintsa and give them things that every day we take for granted.

Passion for Produce
Mary Clay Kline and Reid Mallette

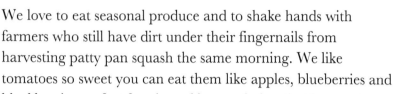

We love to eat seasonal produce and to shake hands with farmers who still have dirt under their fingernails from harvesting patty pan squash the same morning. We like tomatoes so sweet you can eat them like apples, blueberries and blackberries perfect for pie-making, and okra that begs to be dredged in cornmeal and dipped in a fryer.

In the height of sweltering Alabama summers, farmers pile peaches, melons, and sun-ripened tomatoes on folding tables. At 3p.m., we ring the bell, signaling that the Homegrown Alabama Farmers Market is open for business. University students, parents with children, and long-time community residents bustle to their favorite farmer's table to select their weekly produce while melodies from local musicians hum in the background. With harvests so bountiful, we and other patrons are nearly able to avoid grocery stores altogether. Instead of pushing carts through refrigerated buildings, we enjoy our weekly haul on-site, sampling plums and peaches before the market even closes.

Every Thursday, we work to bring farmers from across Alabama together in Tuscaloosa for the only student-run farmers market in the state. Managing a market as full-time college students is hard work, but Homegrown Alabama is a labor of love. If we're lucky, one of the vendors will stop by our tent and drop off a treat for us to try. Dan always shares his strawberries early in the season, and Gary brings us heads of lettuce if he has any left over when the market closes. We love our vendors, and despite the fact that the market rotates through managers as they graduate, we always form close bonds.

The best part of our job is the fact that we get to share our passion for produce with the community. We lounge under our tent on Thursday afternoons and witness the relationships forming between farmers and market patrons as they share produce and stories. It is a privilege for us to provide a platform for vendors to bring farm-fresh goods to Tuscaloosa.

Increasing The Odds
Austin White and Clanesha Munford

Every three minutes, a patient is devastated by the news that they have blood cancer. This prognosis is the start of a long and difficult battle, which, despite the numerous advances in western medicine, still claims over 50,000 lives every year. Fortunately, Be The Match offers a cure by matching healthy bone marrow donors to patients with blood cancers. This selfless act allows the donor to save someone's life. The cure sounds simple: just match a healthy donor with someone with cancer, but getting an exact match that will be accepted by the patient's body is complex and only about 1 in 430 donors will meet this requirement. The only way to increase a patient's odds of finding a match is to increase the pool of healthy donors. Here at the University of Alabama, Be The Match On Campus-UA raises awareness and registers college students to the National Bone Marrow registry, giving young adults the opportunity to be a part of something bigger than themselves and help save the lives of those in need.

Be The Match On Campus-UA is a student run organization, with members who are educating our campus on blood cancers and trying to end the fight against blood cancers, like leukemia and lymphoma, one patient at a time. We are all connected by our drive to help those in need. For some, it was a family member diagnosed with leukemia that started their involvement. They raised awareness by walking in fundraiser

5ks and registering potential donors from their hometown in the hope that someone would be a match for their loved one and donate to save their life. Continuing to college, these members bring that commitment to saving lives and join Be The Match On Campus, in the hopes that no family will feel the devastation that cancer brings.

For other members, their journey with Be The Match started in college. By attending a Be The Match On Campus registration drive, college students hear first-hand accounts of both donors and recipients of the bone marrow donations. At first, donating bone marrow sounds crazy. Learning about the discomfort and risk associated with donating bone marrow is enough to cause anyone to hesitate. However, members of Be The Match provide testimony that the short-term pain and discomfort is worth giving a cure to an individual who would die from blood cancer without their help. We review the support that Be the Match provides the donors by giving those interested the assurance they need to support them to do what they know is right—to take on the risk and responsibility of committing to saving a life and registering to be someone else's cure. This selflessness forever changes many lives when a match is found. The patient and their families get a second chance and the donor family and friends understand the magnitude of the donor's gift. Being a part of that process and being able to touch so many lives is why Be The Match On Campus is our passion.

This piece is written from the perspective of two college kids whose lives continue to be impacted from Be The Match. One student who was a donor and continues to support his recipient, the other who's loved one was saved by a Be The Match bone marrow doner. We are passionate about bone marrow donation and hope to increase the odds of every blood cancer patient. Donation is much more than something being taken from you; it's about the opportunity to give to someone in need.

Lafayette Kids
Isabella Bartels

Along the road through Lafayette Village, there are three speed bumps from the entrance to the Learning Center. *Ready.* The first bump drops away my own concerns about the exam I have next week or the shift I have at work in the morning. *Set.* The second gets me thinking about my students—one needs help catching up on English homework, and I should ask another how his mom and new baby sister are doing. *Go.* The final bump, then we're out of the car and we're on.

As the student lead director of Lafayette Kids, a tutoring and mentoring group for students in a subsidized housing community, the first thing I teach new tutors is how to start building trust. We call ourselves Bigs, and our students Littles. The sibling relationship is powerful in every aspect of our work. After a few weeks, each Big understands how important a trusting adult relationship is for our Littles. All our students get to know us through the community's after-school program. We provide homework help and academic support, but we also have fun Friday activities and outings to explore our town and beyond once a month. None of this would be possible without first building a relationship; the kids have to like us and want to spend time with us first.

Trust extends beyond the relationship between each Big and Little. Equally important is working to build trust with the community we engage in. We need the support of our students' families, our Lafayette Village partners who staff the program, and our students' teachers, and school personnel. If the community trusts us, we can work more effectively at what we do and truly be a fixture in that environment. In my year directing Lafayette Kids, I've aimed much of our focus at building a trusting relationship with our community.

I don't prioritize trust just to make our work easier. I do it because I believe it's a crucial step to any work in education. As a future teacher, and as a current tutor, what I'm most passionate about is connecting the dots between education programs and the communities they exist in. I've found that the communities I've worked in are a unique and impossibly valuable source of information, support, and cooperation. If my work in community service is going to be in any way impactful, I must first learn to engage with and learn from the community.

Lisa Delpit, one of my most idolized educators, reminds us that we are experts in nothing but our own lives. At Lafayette Kids, I started as an outsider coming into a community I knew nothing about. The world of Virginia public schools, of subsidized housing, and of my students' families was not one I shared. Though I've been working with these students for three years now, I still (and probably always will) have a lot to learn. I can read as many articles and take as many classes as I want, but I believe the most effective way to learn about education in a particular community is from that community itself. And, if the community is going to teach me what I need to know, they have to first trust me. They have to trust that I want the best for their students. Trust that I will work diligently to support their students. Trust that I am engaged, I care, and I will be as much a part of the community as they allow me to be.

81

The Passions of a Beekeeper
Madison Ruff

A simple New Year's resolution was the inspiration for a new hobby. In an effort to expand my passions, I opened myself up to new opportunities. I was not yet looking for my new hobby when it found me. I signed up for a beekeeping class at the University of North Carolina Wilmington (UNCW) just for fun. I had previously done a research project on honey and was fascinated by bees and wanted a deeper understanding of their way of life. In the class, I learned just how important bees are to our way of life.

If bees were to go extinct, global food production would be cut by a third. Bees not only supply direct sources of food, like fruits and vegetables, but they indirectly supply our food as well. By pollinating grasses and flowers, bees are providing a food source for the animals we eat. Honeybees face hardships such as Colony Collapse Disorder (CCD), where honeybees abandon hives full of larva and honey. This is highly unusual and there are no definite explanations as to why this phenomenon is happening. I want to do my part to help the honeybee population any way I can. As I monitor my own hives, I will also be able to offer any research I can to help find solutions to problems such as CCD.

My love for honey alone could honestly drive my passion for beekeeping. Nothing in this world beats buttered toast and honey. Unfortunately, if honeybees go extinct, they would take their honey with them. Honey is the ultimate super food and can be used in everything from medicine to beauty products. A world without honey would be a bitter place.

Even though honeybees are amazingly industrious with their honey production, if I were to describe honeybees in a single word, it would have to be quirky. Describing an insect as quirky may seem a little strange, but they obsess over imperfections, are impressively tidy, have a specific way to do everything, and dance to communicate. Bees have millions of quirks about them, which honestly makes me love them even more.

My passion for beekeeping is ultimately driven by the overall importance of honeybees, honey, and the bees themselves. I have devoted myself to saving the bees, and that is exactly what I plan to do.

All For Autism
Hannah Collins

Autism Spectrum Disorder (ASD) affects 1 in 68 children, making it one of the fastest growing developmental disorders in the US today. ASD does not know race, ethnicity, or social class. Children and adults from all backgrounds are diagnosed with ASD, and the developmental delays brought on by the disorder cost families tens of thousands of dollars each year. There are many organizations that support families affected by ASD such as Autism Speaks, which runs events throughout April for Autism Awareness Month and throughout the entire year in order to advocate for ASD. Operating out of Purdue University, a student run organization, All For Autism focuses on advocating and educating students and the community about autism through fundraisers.

Children and adults on the autism spectrum have many desirable traits, such as great memory skills and visuo-spatial skills. They generally have a better outlook on life being less materialistic and having a whole lot of passion for others. Unfortunately, the many benefits are eclipsed by societal norms that make it difficult for someone with ASD to grow in a society that does not understand the disorder. Autism can be accompanied by problematic behaviors as a result of not getting basic wants and needs met. Imagine listening to a teacher in class and spotting a board game across the room. While walking over to the game, the teacher voices the student to remain seated. Playing the board game with friends is the main desire in that moment, not listening to a teacher talking about mathematics. As a result, frustration builds and manifests into an outburst. This is a huge interruption to the educational process for someone with ASD. It is devastating to witness the lack of understanding among educators in regards to autism and the techniques that are required to accommodate those students. Thankfully, methods of decreasing problematic behaviors and teaching educators those methods have been developed by researchers, making it easier for children with ASD to be a part of a classroom. One of the many talents someone on the autism spectrum has is enhanced visuo-spatial skills. In the classroom, curriculums are being put in place to take advantage of those skills—for instance, giving each child a visual schedule to follow with pictures of what they will be doing throughout the day. This curriculum helps the students with ASD to be engaged with learning new material without having anxiety about what is coming next. Therefore, it is taking one of autism's strengths and eliminating a weakness, allowing the child to be more successful.

This excites the members of All For Autism at Purdue University and autism advocates across the country because it shows that the world is evolving into a more autism friendly place. Always remember, different, not less.

Veterinary Exotic Animal Club
Kelsey Trumpp

❖

When most people are asked the question, "What does a veterinarian do?" they respond by describing a medical professional who cares for domesticated animals, especially pets or farm animals. Rarely do they consider those who have dedicated their careers to the health and preservation of non-domestic species, including free-ranging and captive wildlife populations. However, these veterinarians are an ever-growing fraction of the profession. With a changing climate and many other problems increasingly affecting the ability of wildlife to survive on their own, the need for veterinarians in this specialty can only be expected to increase.

I, along with many of my colleagues, have a strong and growing interest in the medicine of wildlife, including endangered species. This is a field that requires a large amount of creativity and innovation, as the anatomy, physiology, and behavior of so many animals are not yet fully understood. There are significant research opportunities within this field as well, allowing for exploration and expression of new ideas. However, it is not just wild animal species that fall under the scope of conservation-minded veterinarians. Many of us are also drawn to the concept of One Health, which incorporates the health of the environment, humans, and non-human animals into a singular goal. This approach allows us to network with professionals in other fields and look past the scope of veterinary medicine alone.

My passion for wildlife and the conservation of endangered species has grown through multiple personal experiences. The lens through which I view the world has also inspired me to pursue my chosen career path. I have always been fascinated with nature and the way in which humans and non-human animals interact. My parents made sure I spent time outside when I was younger and instilled a love and curiosity for the natural world in me. When I began looking for an undergraduate program of study, I knew that I wanted to pursue animal behavior as my major. Instead of focusing on animal behavior in isolation, I chose to pursue a degree in Animal Behavior, Ecology, and Conservation that allowed me to connect what I was learning to the interactions between all living things. I was able to travel to places like South Africa and Hawaii to study not only animal behavior, but human-animal interactions and conservation strategies. These experiences made me passionate about the animals we share this planet with and inspired me to strive to improve the conditions for wildlife species around the globe.

My desire to help animals in a tangible way led me to veterinary school. I entered knowing that I wanted to dedicate my career to caring for and increasing our understanding of endangered species. With this passion driving my decisions, I knew that I had to find a way to incorporate exotic animal medicine into my time as a veterinary student, even though it was rarely taught in the curriculum. I recognized the passion of my fellow students as well. Our combined desire to learn about non-domestic animal medicine has led to the continued development of extracurricular opportunities that allow for the development of technical skills and applicable knowledge that we can use later in our career. Throughout my time as a veterinary student, I have discovered that I am not only passionate about conservation and endangered species, but that I also enjoy helping my future colleagues discover opportunities to get involved in this unique area of veterinary medicine. I realized that diversity is not just critically important in the natural world, but also among the voices of my colleagues as we work toward a common goal. Teaching and leadership have become an important part of my journey to become the best conservation-focused veterinarian I can be.

My passion for wildlife and the conservation of endangered species has guided me on my path to becoming a veterinarian. It has allowed me to network with my peers and future colleagues. I have found ways to provide learning opportunities for others, while also improving my own knowledge base and skills. Becoming an exotic animal veterinarian is my passion because it allows me to use my technical knowledge while also expressing my creative side, allows me to help shape a community of like-minded yet diverse professionals, and provides me with a constant opportunity to make a positive difference in the lives of multiple animal species and the humans who care so deeply for them.

Ms. Brightside
Emily Beth Goldstein

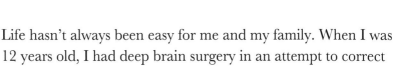

Life hasn't always been easy for me and my family. When I was 12 years old, I had deep brain surgery in an attempt to correct a genetic neurological movement disorder. If you don't know what that means, basically doctors put batteries in my chest and wires in my brain to help me walk. Without this, I would certainly be in a wheelchair today and I don't know if I would have had the physical independence to move across the country from a suburb of Los Angeles, California, to attend the University of Alabama. Despite this hardship, my family remained strong and positive and we always looked on the bright side of the darkest times. This was especially true when my older brother, Adam, was diagnosed with Stage 4 Hodgkin's Lymphoma in October of my sophomore year of college. Even with this devastating diagnosis, we never thought Adam was going to die. I always assumed that, like me, his luck would turn around and he would be magically cured of cancer. Sadly, that did not happen. After many chemotherapy treatments, which did not work, and trying a new, innovative immunotherapy drug, which also did not work, my family was left hopeless and confused when Adam passed away at age 23, just six short months after his initial diagnosis.

Ironically, about a month before my brother's initial diagnosis, I was selected to be a founding co-director of a new chapter of a program I had never heard of: Camp Kesem.

Camp Kesem is a national non-profit organization with a mission to help all kids who have been impacted by their parents' cancer. In addition to year-round fundraising, we organize a week-long camp for these kids to escape their problems and to help them feel like normal kids again. When I first joined Kesem, I didn't really have a very strong connection to the mission, other than the fact that I simply like kids and serving others. Now, however, I am connected to the mission more so than ever. I love Kesem because it allows these kids to see the brightness in a dark situation. These kids have to grow up so quickly, sometimes even by taking on the role of the adult at such a young age. I know how hard it was for me to deal with my brother's cancer and I couldn't even imagine how difficult it would be if I were younger and even more vulnerable.

So, when asked what I am passionate about, I have a couple answers. I am passionate about positivity and looking on the bright side of life. I am passionate about my brother and making sure that I live my life to honor him. But, most importantly, I am passionate about service and helping others. I understand how hard it is to be positive during the most difficult times of life. So, if I can help someone else and make their hard times just a little bit easier and happier, I'll try my very hardest.

Engineering World Health
Anonymous

Each one of us knows someone who has been affected by a disease in varying degrees. It's something that touches our everyday lives and leaves damage in its wake. That's why so many young men and women have the passion to help people and their families suffering from diseases.

The constant innovation of medicine and medical devices allows for cures of disease to spread around the world. These solutions can then be refined to reach the farthest villages at an affordable cost. This passage harnesses our passion for using collegiate engineering to improve healthcare around the world. The ambition to make an impact on people's lives through improvement of the medical field is shared by all peers of this organization.

Our passion for helping others and improving healthcare drives the mission of Engineering World Health. As engineering students, we are lucky to learn critical thinking and problem solving to address the current issues that developing countries face when it comes to medicine. Our mindset allows us to creatively approach a problem and brainstorm how the medical solution could be made cheaper, more efficiently, and how it could be better implemented in a third world country. We are able to apply what we learn in the classroom to find workable solutions through innovation and creativity. The design competitions of Engineering World Health inspire us to renovate and create simple improvements to medical equipment for under-resourced areas. Turning our ideas into actual devices is empowering and further encourages us to pursue helping out the global healthcare scene.

Not only are the logistics of the problem analyzed, but the impact of the work is too. This organization allows us to pursue any project we want and offers us advice to improve our design. Engineering can improve the human condition in all aspects of life and we can tailor it to improve healthcare. It gives us the opportunity to reach out and impact people of all ages and from all walks of life.

When one hears about the outbreaks and sufferings from disease around the world, it is only human nature to want to extend a hand and help. Engineering World Health allows fresh minded, determined collegiate students like ourselves to improve global healthcare in our own way and gives us a taste of true engineering. It also is an eye-opening way for collegiate students to truly see the impact their work can have on patients in need.

How Anthropologists Shape Our World
Megan Street

We have lost count of how many times we have been called Indiana Jones, or asked if we have found any dinosaurs yet. Every now and then, we fend off our families' concerns about our choice of not-always-so-lucrative work. Anthropology continues to be one of the most misunderstood—and perhaps most untapped—branches of science. It is simultaneously the most humanistic of the sciences, and the most scientific of the humanities. It is where facts and emotions co-exist rather than clash. Simply put, we study people, from everyday mundane interactions to how we view our individual places in the vast world we inhabit.

I grew up in rural America, where the people are good-natured but of similar morals and backgrounds. Hardly anything challenges the status quo and outsiders are met with apprehension, at the very least. Fear of the unknown is what anthropologists counter: the goal is not to push people to change, but instead to give them the tools to learn from one another. I have also witnessed firsthand the hardships of poverty that anthropologists working in development strive to combat and fix for a long time to come. It was these questions about the outside world that drove me to explore what I felt I had been missing. I wanted to explore who I was, who I could be, and what I could learn from those different from myself.

The attractive thing about anthropology is the sheer number of ways we can use it. Most people, as mentioned before, picture us as archaeologists sifting through dirt to find artifacts of some long-lost culture. And yes, this is what some anthropologists do, but that percentage is rather small. A huge number work in business, government, forensics, IT, and even the fine arts. Others become political and social activists or politicians. Even more stay in education to pass on the tools of our trade to the next generation. This medley of professions has grown just about as diverse as the very people we study.

Increasingly present in our discourse is the question of whether or not anthropologists should become advocates where they have been neutral scholars, putting ourselves on the front lines of change rather than peering at it from behind a computer screen. Traditionally, like most scientists, anthropologists sought to remain emotionally removed from our work to avoid bias, but the very nature of what we do often immerses us deeply in the very issues we try so hard to document. A newer generation of scholars is beginning to embrace the way their personal identities are intertwined with their interests, and is exploring how they can create change in their own communities.

However, as vast as our careers are, in no way does it dilute the knowledge we have gathered. In an interconnected, globalized world that becomes smaller every day, yet one that seems increasingly chaotic and split, anthropologists offer an impartial view of human diversity and identity that is often difficult for people on the inside of situations to see. We tend to be gatekeepers where social divides exist. Wherever we might end up, our shared passion and love for our fellow human beings is what drives us forward.

Caring For Camo
Allison Kim Huynh

Today was hard. I failed my biology test, which I deserved. It has been rainy and cold all month. Gross. I went home and answered some emails, surfed through social media, and planned to take a nap. I was pretty tired after trying to remember what my professor discussed on polar nuclei in plant reproductive systems when I half-listened in class. Another $1,000 university class thrown out the window. It's fine.

My mom called me, asking if I was coming home for dinner. I scrambled together an excuse to get out of the 15 minute drive and the 30 minute family "bonding" time. I'm in college now, why would I want to go home? She hung up the phone, disappointed yet again.

Three days later, a friend from the past texted me. "Hey, just wanted to catch up… I love college! Can't wait to join organizations, which do you think I should do?" I didn't answer. Maybe I should start getting involved.

Where to begin…

Caring For Camo (CFC) is a student led non-profit organization that started at the University of Texas (UT), Austin in 2012. Since then, it has expanded to three other schools: the University of Alabama, Central Florida, and Wisconsin. The main mission of the organization is to send letters and care packages to troops in the United States Armed

Forces. CFC does so by hosting bi-annual "packing parties", where the UT and Austin community come together to write personal letters and assemble boxes of supplies for soldiers. At every event, we ship about 250 boxes that reach 4-50 troops— that's at least 1,000 soldiers.

I stumbled upon Caring For Camo by accident when I was looking through the 2000+ organizations on my university website. By mid-semester, it was too late to get involved with many organizations till Spring so my choices were limited. I emailed CFC asking to join, and, to my surprise, was asked to fill out a form for an officer position. This opportunity seemed too good. I went to my interview, got the position as Development Chair, and was thrown into the world of non-profit organizations and the struggles of building one.

I had barely been introduced into the organization before I was drowned by the financial issues. I learned quickly that the non-profit was struggling to uphold their core purpose to send packages due to one big roadblock: funding. For the whole of my first year working with CFC, my duty as Development Chair officer was to find ways to fund our "packing parties". I spent countless hours researching and emailing companies and made enough cold-calls to memorize my speech. Instead of my hourly naps during class, my head was buried behind my computer screen searching for any penny I could gain for CFC. The organization had finally gathered enough to host the first packing party of my year.

A few months later, I was appointed the position of president for the new year. I stumbled upon a folder marked "soldiers responses" and started reading through some old letters. I was immediately filled with a bittersweet feeling. To see how far and powerful our reach was, and to feel the impact we made was amazing. But, to read about the struggles soldiers face and to see how little they had was painful. The worst part of Caring For Camo was the guilt. The guilt I felt after learning that many of these soldiers, some my age, couldn't go through the same "college life". The guilt of avoiding the time I was blessed enough to have with my family. The guilt that I took all I had and all I was given for granted. Caring For Camo made me realize there was more to care about than myself. I had to look beyond my selfish struggles and open my eyes to what others needed. Caring For Camo made me find myself and my passion.

So what am I passionate about?

I am passionate about life. I am passionate about caring. And, I am passionate about using what I have to help those who don't have anything. Caring For Camo allows me to support my passions while sharing with others why we should all have more than 1,000 reasons to care.

Lost and Found
Kylie Johnson

Lost and Found is a suicide awareness and prevention non-profit organization with a focus on college students. The original chapter formed at the University of South Dakota in 2011 and the second chapter was created at South Dakota State University shortly after. With humble beginnings as a simple student organization on two university campuses, a lot of expansion and growth has occurred over the last few years.

Numerous college students in South Dakota have joined forces to work toward a common purpose: to prevent suicide and depression around the globe; to help colleges continue to provide free counseling and/or medication to students dealing with depression; and to raise money for families affected by attempted or completed suicide.

Passion is a driving force for the members of Lost and Found's suicide awareness and prevention movement. All members fully embrace the purpose of this non-profit organization. Members put their entire heart into all of our activities, whether they are big or small. Each semester, members are trained through the "Question, Persuade, and Refer" method in order to recognize suicide warning signs and be informed on how to respond in high-risk situations. They utilize this knowledge in situations if needed, and have the ability to encourage people with suicidal thoughts to get the help they need. Furthermore, each year, both chapters hold different fundraisers within the community to raise money for our purpose. These funds provide students with the opportunity to help families in need and promote our organization on campus so that students know where they can go for support.

Starting a conversation about suicide prevention is difficult, but necessary. Discussing other options and spreading hope can impact the lives of others and prevent them from committing the act of suicide. By being passionate about this, Lost and Found is impacting not only students on campus, but also people within the community, and eventually around the globe. Students are working against the negative stigma surrounding suicide and mental health. It is okay to not be okay, but it is important to take the necessary steps in order to get better, which is what Lost and Found promotes.

The future of our organization is looking bright. Currently, Lost and Found is trying to transition into having more in-depth training for the executive board and all active members. Additionally, we are looking into starting support groups for students on campus who have been affected by suicide. This will allow people who are all passionate about this movement to work together and support one another.

Then Feed Just One
Josie Galles and Krayton Schnepf

Since we were kindergarteners at our school, we have been participating in a large packing event called Then Feed Just One (TFJO). We came to realize that these events were for a good cause, but we never grasped that making the meals could save someone's life. This realization led us down a road of trying to make the world a better place.

Our first step was to venture to a third world country: Honduras. As seniors at Gehlen Catholic High School in Le Mars, IA, we had the opportunity to be a part of something bigger than ourselves. As we stepped off our plane, traveled to our village on the outskirts of Nueva Capital, our eyes were immediately opened to the sufferings and troubles of poverty. As we continued up the hill to the school we would be staying at, we saw children running around with no shoes, covered in dirt and mud, and so skinny you would think they were three years younger than they were. The kids swarmed all of us students as we got off our bus; their eyes shone with gratitude and love. While down there, we built three houses, a garden, ten bunkbeds, and delivered gift bags filled with shoes, clothes, soaps, toothbrushes, and so much more. As we were delivering bags, we even got to witness a family eat our TFJO food packaged at Gehlen.

This was the most humbling experience any of us had gone through. On our last night in Honduras, Richard Seivert, the founder of TFJO and Gehlen Mission Honduras, sent us an email. Part of it said, "Don't wait for others to do it, change could and might be you."

Well, we took this message to heart. We returned to our, what a Honduran considered, "luxurious" life, but we kept our simplicity and love of the Honduran culture with us. Neither Krayton nor I wanted to forget our experiences, our emotions, from Honduras. We have both said we went into Honduras thinking we were going to change lives. We didn't expect them to change ours. Each day, we miss being with our friends in Honduras, and we have decided to do something for them here since we cannot be there.

We ended up going to the same college, the University of South Dakota, and decided to put into action the message we wanted to spread. We contacted Richard Seivert and Carolyn Bickford (retired teachers from Gehlen that direct Gehlen Mission Honduras and TFJO), and together, we started the University of South Dakota's Then Feed Just One. We made a constitution, contacted members to be a part of our board, and started brainstorming. Our goal is to host packaging events in the fall and spring, but also to educate others on third world poverty. We hosted a mini packing event on April 19, 2017 and it was a huge success. Thinking we would only pack 5,000 meals, our fellow peers packaged close to 12,000. It was a dream come true. We were able to spread the word of poverty, and educates those on how we can help alleviate it.

Packing events consist of volunteers donating their time and money. TFJO must pay for the food it packs. The food in each bag consists of whole grains, rice, vegetable mixes, and chicken powder. Each ingredient is chosen for its nutrition. Four people dump these ingredients into a bag through a funnel. After the bag is full, it is moved to the weighing station. Each bag weighs to about 13.8 ounces. From the weighing station, it proceeds to the sealing station. The most important part of this is to make sure all the air is out of the bag so no more weight is added. Each TFJO bag consists of six meals. Each meal costs sixteen cents.

Many people do not realize how easy it is to help. A simple donation, a helping hand, a loving prayer, anything an individual does through the kindness of their heart is all that is needed. A large pizza can feed thirty people. A coffee from Starbucks can feed five people. A prayer sent as a gift, well, it can save a life.

The Mars Society, Indiana Chapter
Kshitij Mall

The past is the best reminder of mistakes that should never be repeated in our present that could destroy our future. A single planet species is doomed to extinction. Dinosaurs got wiped off the face of this blue world because they could not launch themselves to another safer world when their time of peril dawned. A similar fate lies ahead of humanity if we don't learn from this past about our planet.

We humans have been wanderers and nomadic for most of our tenure on the planet. Our curiosity to know where we came from and where we are heading propels us from one destination to the next. Humanity was, is, and will always be plagued with many issues, but that will never curb our curiosity to know the unknown and to discover the hidden. The same happened when Europeans started to search for India and ended up finding America. There was poverty, there were health issues, and so on, but nothing stopped these brave explorers from venturing into the expanse of vast oceans with a myriad of dangers. America, the new home of many humans, was discovered and is rightly called the Land of Opportunities.

These facts are the proponents of space exploration by humans and the search for our next homes. The next most logical destination to serve as our home is Mars. It would serve as the next baby step that we take toward space exploration. It would be very different from a human mission to the moon as it would not be just about leaving footsteps and flags behind, but to start a new human race together who would be called Martians—the people of the red world.

Just thinking about going to our next home is the first step of the entire journey. To reach the destination, we would need to start working right now. School students need to be taught about the basic skills that would be needed to setup their new homes and survive on the red world. All those who are working on different aspects of Mars need to work together to solve challenges confronting humanity in this conquest of a new planet.

Purdue University, popularly known as the cradle of astronauts, is currently the epicenter of Mars related research. Much research is being conducted on aerospace systems, astrodynamics, material science, geology, agriculture, bio-medical science, and human factors, to name a few. In order to unite these forces working at Purdue, we formed the Mars Society Purdue Chapter. We are also conducting outreach activities to educate and inspire young students at various elementary schools in Indiana. We share exciting opportunities with university students regarding Mars related competitions and Purdue has won top prizes globally. We also formed a team for a Mars Desert Research Station that got selected among top ten teams in the world to perform a Mars analog mission at the end of 2017. Our organization is thus able to make a significant impact and work toward building our next home on Mars.

A time will soon arrive when being an astronaut is commonplace. The red world would be terraformed to another blue-green world filled with various life forms. We humans are the brand ambassadors and insurance agents of life. Hence, it is our duty to embark upon this exciting journey to our next home and to spread beautiful life beyond this blue world. It will take some time for us to make this dream come true, but it will happen. We at the Mars Society Purdue Chapter work toward this beautiful and optimistic goal of humanity in our own capacity and this is what we are passionate about. To Mars and beyond!

LWA&A
Ben Christiansen

My name is Ben Christiansen and I have ADHD. Growing up, I always had a constant struggle with focusing, whether it was with school, chores, or even reading about things I had a deep interest in. During my middle school and high school years, I started caring less and less about my school work and focused more on putting in just enough effort to scrape by. When high school graduation rolled around, I wasn't even sure if college was something for me to pursue, and considered taking an alternate route for my post-graduation path. However, I started my first semester at the University of Alabama and ended up making straight A's for the first time in my life. Though, I felt like I had accomplished something good, I noticed that most people around me were able to achieve the same thing without having to put in near as much time and effort. I decided to start paying attention to my habits, behaviors, and the attitudes of my everyday life. I realized how much I had neglected cultivating good habits and didn't avoid developing the bad ones. During the summer after my sophomore year, I realized how far I had progressed in managing my ADHD. It had also occurred to me that I could share what I had done with others who also struggle with the condition. When I found there was no organization on campus that was specifically oriented towards bringing together those who have ADD or ADHD, I decided to create one and named it Living with ADD and

ADHD (LWA&A). LWA&A is an organization that aims to educate others about what can be done to manage ADD and ADHD symptoms. Each time the organization meets, a different topic is discussed. Topics range from eating and sleeping habits to stress management and relaxation techniques. By the time I had reached this point in my life, I realized that I had developed a passion for mental health and developing a positive outlook on life when trying to overcome ADHD. Understanding my mental health made the difference between completing a task or being overwhelmed by it. It is the difference between life being worth living, and not. I have found it to be fulfilling to help others realize they can overcome the symptoms of ADD and ADHD, and that they can help others do the same.

Gerontology
Madison Lewis

When asked what I am studying or what my career path is, and when I tell whoever is inquiring, their face changes into an expression of confusion. First off, not many people can define "gerontology" and when I tell them they say, "Why would you want to work with old people?" My response to them is, "Well, why not?" Gerontology and the aging population is not just taking care of dying people who are at the worst point in their lives. In fact, the preparation for retirement, having conversations about quality of life at a vulnerable point for some, providing some of the best care for older adults, and insuring their safety and happiness are a few of the things that gerontologists strive to gain knowledge about.

The desire to care for people struck me at a young age. My paternal great grandmother lived with us for a summer when I was just 14 years old. I was not able to drive yet and I lived in a rural area so seeing friends was difficult. Over those three months, my great grandmother became my best friend—not something I would ever expect.

Becoming a caregiver at just age 14 sparked my passion for older adults and I was not made aware of this passion until my junior year of college when I took a Gerontology 201 class. We were required to do service learning which involved volunteering at an assisted living facility. There, I was exposed to the love and friendliness that older adults embodied and how much they enjoyed someone to be with them.

My professor at James Madison University fed my passion for older adults as well. Sitting in her lectures, I could feel a sense of belonging. That is when I decided my career path needed to be working with older adults. After my undergraduate work, I decided to pursue a Master's degree in Applied Gerontology at the University of North Carolina, Wilmington.

Many people who work in geriatrics stumble across this profession. To my surprise, I did not know how much I enjoyed, and I would even say, needed older adults in my life. Being able to create a profession out of the love in my heart is why I love being a gerontologist.

Older adults need advocates, which is an important factor to being a gerontologist. Listening to their needs and understanding the dynamic between family members and an older adult is key. Society has created a stigma that aging is gloomy and lonely. The media portrays "ageism", which is defined by sociologists as a negative reputation of people based on their age. The fact that we do not admire and respect our older adults is why these viewpoints have been created. Being able to ensure quality of life for those who cannot advocate for themselves is why I am passionate about gerontology.

Working in a place surrounded by older adults creates an energetic and ever-changing environment. I thrive off never having the same exact work day, day in and day out. My "customers" are the residents of whatever environment I am working in and they love to share their stories with me. My favorite part of being a gerontologist is learning from my residents. Their lives are so important to their wellbeing, so taking the time to get to know them is key in this profession.

Gerontology is an underappreciated profession but I am so thankful to be part of it every day. I have always wanted to help people and being able to touch the lives of many older adults is a blessing. If I could tell the world one thing, it would be to get to know the older adults in your life. Not only will they enrich your life, you will be enriching theirs. Ask about their families or what they did before they retired. Be a listener. Be an advocate. And, most of all, be a lover.

About Z Publishing

❖

Begun as a blog in the fall of 2015, Z Publishing, LLC, is currently transitioning into book publishing. This transition is in response to the problem plaguing the publishing world: For writers, finding new readers can be tremendously difficult, and for readers, finding new, talented authors with whom they identify is like finding a needle in a haystack. With Z Publishing, no one will have to go about this process alone any more. By producing anthologies of multiple authors rather than single-author volumes, Z Publishing hopes to harbor a community of readers and writers, bringing all sides of the industry closer together.

To sign up for the Z Publishing newsletter or to submit your own writing to a future anthology, visit www.zpublishinghouse.com.

You can also follow the evolution of Z Publishing on the following platforms:

Facebook: www.facebook.com/zpublishing

Twitter: www.twitter.com/z_publishing

Author Biographies
(In Order of Appearance)

Mayank Mehta: Mayank is an undergraduate student at the University of Illinois in Urbana Champaign. As an aspiring filmmaker, he hopes to tell stories that can raise empathy and love within humanity in hopes of creating a brighter future for everyone.

Gabriela Lozano Flores: Born and raised in Monterrey, Mexico, Gabbie currently attends the University of Iowa pursing a Bachelor of Science in Microbiology. Gabbie is planning on pursuing a Master's of Public Health in the future and eventually attending medical school.

Maggie Brennan: Maggie is a current sophomore at the University of Wisconsin-Madison and co-president of the university's Undergraduate Advocacy for Human Rights with Mica Beckmann. Outside of this organization, she participates on the Wisconsin Alumni Student Board and tries to make it to as many live shows Madison has to offer with her free time!

Taylor Majher: Taylor is a junior at the University of Iowa majoring in Human Physiology, and president of the student service organization, Circle K. He is also a current Patient

Escort at the University of Iowa Hospitals and Clinics and prospective FoodCorps volunteer.

Sarah Mohammed Murad: Sarah is a biology major at George Washington University in Washington, D.C. She is from Kuwait and is pursuing a medical degree. She is the president of the Global Brigades Chapter and is excited to send her first brigade to Nicaragua this year.

Hasan Nadeem: Hasan is currently president and co-founder of We're Better Than That - Men Against Sexual Assault at UW-Madison. The group aims to educate and engage the male student population to first recognize the issue of sexual violence as a humanitarian issue, to further acknowledge the role men play in the issue, and to ultimately shape men as ambassadors in the call to end sexual violence. Facebook: https://www.facebook.com/wbttmasa/. Website: https://wbttblog.wordpress.com/.

Ellyson Rae Martens: Ellyson is a sophomore biomedical engineering student at the University of Iowa. She became involved with Continental Crossings as a freshman and will be traveling to Nicaragua in the summer of 2017.

Malaney Young: Malaney is secretary of NAMI on Campus UMN

Sohan Phadke and Ruthvik Hejibu: Sohan and Ruthvik are students at the University of Minnesota-Twin Cities. Since they were little, both have attended Chinmaya Mission, a non-profit Sunday school teaching Hindu religion, culture, and Indian languages. They are excited to share the Hindu culture they have experienced through India trips to see family, speaking Indian languages at home, and through Chinmaya Mission.

Marissa Plescia: Marissa is a freshman at the University of Illinois pursuing a Bachelor's Degree in Journalism. She is the Editor in Chief for the club, Brands Give Back, an organization that combines fashion with sustainability.

Victor Lopez: Victor is currently a sophomore at the University of Illinois Urbana-Champaign studying Food Science with Chemistry. Since high school, he has acquired over 500 service hours and has received multiple Presidential Volunteer Awards through his involvement with the non-profit organization buildOn. His devotion to buildOn and its ideal of service has devoted him to start a Chapter of buildOn at his university and is currently the president of the buildOn Chapter at UIUC. He plans to lead his team to raise money in order to build a school for one of the many developing countries that buildOn is associated with, and also give his members the opportunity to find their passion through many service opportunities.

Lindsey Knox: Lindsey is a fourth year student at the University of Minnesota College of Veterinary Medicine. She has always had a connection with humans and animals, which led her to pursue a career in veterinary medicine with a specific interest in shelter medicine. She is incredibly humbled to be able to share her passion of health and wellness and hopes to spark the same interest in you as the reader.

Marcus Miller: Marcus is a student at the University of Iowa studying political science, and ethics and public policy. With the help of Sarah Henry and the Sanctuary Community Church, Marcus formed a campus ministry called Love Works, which officially launched the Spring of 2017. The campus ministry seeks to provide a space for all to talk about a variety of different issues, such as social justice, faith, and how to connect with God and the world around us.

Susan Metzger and Benjamin Harbst: Susan and Benjamin are currently fourth year medical students at the University of Minnesota. They are currently pursuing careers in psychiatry and physical medicine and rehabilitation, respectively. In their free time, both enjoy spinning vinyl records and researching aspects of integrative medicine. Both are life-long laughers.

Meghan Hill and Tatiana Lyons: Meghan and Tatiana are juniors at the University of Minnesota-Twin Cities. Both are founding members of Jewish Community Action at the University of Minnesota. They are passionate about engaging the Jewish community in social justice work, such as criminal justice reform.

Andrea Poppinga: Andrea is a 20-year-old student at Iowa State University.

Sydney Paysheninne: Sydney is a Saginaw Chippewa/Sauk anishinaabe kwe (woman). Sydney graduated with a BBA in marketing during April 2017, and has done various environmental work during her time as an undergrad at Eastern Michigan. Being president of the Native American Student Organization (NASO) at EMU (Fall/Winter 2017) allowed her to make various connections, state wide and beyond, with other Native American Student Organizations. This also extends to environmental networks that share common interests of protecting the environment and creating a safe cultural space for students. Sydney can be reached at sskaggs@emich.edu.

Greg Brooks JR: Greg is the Youngstown State NSBE Chapter president.

Amy Olejniczak: Amy is a student at the College of William & Mary, in Williamsburg, Virginia. She is excited to share the power of handwritten positivity and encouragement with individuals on campus, in the local community, and all over the world.

Camille Mero: Camille is a freshman studying physiology at the University of Arizona. This year, Camille has become a part of A Moment of Magic, a non-profit organization dedicated to visiting children in the oncology unit with efforts of making their day a little more magical. She is excited to use her efforts in building a chapter at the University of Arizona to extend the organization throughout Southern Arizona.

Kelsey Hennig: Kelsey received her Bachelor's Degree in Addiction Studies and Psychology from the University of South Dakota. She is currently working towards her Master's in Clinical Mental Health Counseling at the University of Northern Colorado. She is excited to see where her studies will take her and how she will be able to help others.

Morgan Clark: Morgan is a senior at the University of North Carolina Wilmington. She holds a BA in Spanish Language and is in the BS in Nursing program. She serves on the advisory board for the non-profit Curamericas and is the founder and president of Make A Change.

Reed Trende and Drake Krohn: Reed and Drake are students at Purdue University in West Lafayette, Indiana. Though neither have food-related majors, their upbringings and volunteering experiences helped cultivate their passion for the hungry. They were able to continue to pursue their passion for hunger at Purdue through Swipe Out Starvation, a student organization seeking to minimize food waste in the campus dining courts.

Arianna Barley: Arianna is a senior at the University of Alabama. During her freshman year, she adopted a vegan lifestyle, and in her sophomore year, she created Vegan Voices, a university organization that works toward the betterment of animal and environmental welfare, and she has acted as the president of the organization ever since. https://www.facebook.com/uavegans/.

Jamaica Cooper: Jamaica is an advocate for those with disabilities who also travels to speak and share her personal experience of living with a disability. Jamaica is also a writer and a poet and hopes to publish her autobiography within the next two years. For more information, you can email Jamaica at Jamaicacooper64@gmail.com.

Christian Pollema: Christian is a student at the University of South Dakota. He was first involved in SERVE during his first year, volunteering for both Adopt-A-Grandparent and Big Pal Little Pal. During his second year, he served as the co-chair for the Big Pal Little Pal program, and will be serving as SERVE's overall president for the 2017-2018 academic year. He is passionate about SERVE and promoting active citizenship, and believes that an effective community is a cohesive community.

Christopher James Santos: Christopher is currently a senior majoring in Marketing and Supply Chain Management with a minor in Africana Studies at Binghamton University. To learn more about Helping Chintsa, please email helpingchintsa@binghamtonsa.org.

Mary Clay Kline and Reid Mallette: Mary Clay and Reid are seniors at the University of Alabama. As life-long southerners, they were raised to appreciate local produce and home cooking. Mary Clay is a journalism major and line cook who thinks about food almost obsessively. Reid is studying to become a chemical engineer and loves gardening and cooking for her friends and family.

Austin White and Clanesha Munford: Austin and Clanesha are students at the University of Alabama and are the president and secretary of Be The Match On Campus-UA. Clanesha's journey started after a family member was diagnosed with leukemia, while Austin donated bone marrow twice for a man with leukemia and is applying to medical school this year based on this experience.

Isabella Bartels: Isabella is a senior at the College of William and Mary from Staten Island, New York. She is studying English, Secondary Education, and ESL Education, and hopes to one day be a New York City public high school principal. Isabella loves exploring New York, strong coffee, and working with kids.

Madison Ruff: Madison is a student at the University of North Carolina, Wilmington, and majoring in Environmental Studies. She is currently the president of the UNCW Beekeepers and has the beginnings of her own personal apiary. She intends on continuing beekeeping after college and potentially making a career out of it.

Hannah Collins: Hannah studies Speech, Language, and Hearing Sciences at Purdue University and hopes to continue with a Doctorate in Audiology. Currently, she is the president of All For Autism at Purdue and helps in a lab that teaches educators techniques that help children with autism succeed.

Kelsey Trumpp: Kelsey received her B.S. degree in Animal Behavior, Ecology, and Conservation from Canisius College in 2015. She is currently a third year veterinary student at Purdue University where she is the president of the Veterinary Exotic Animal Club. Kelsey plans on pursuing a specialty certification from the American College of Zoological Medicine after graduation. She is passionate about conservation medicine and One Health and intends to make a difference for endangered species throughout her career as a veterinarian. Kelsey may be contacted at ktrumpp@purdue.edu.

Emily Beth Goldstein: Emily Beth is a junior at the University of Alabama studying Human Development and Family Studies, with a concentration in Child Life. Although she loves child life, her passion and hope for the future is to study medicine as it combines her love for science, life-long learning, and serving others. In her free time, Emily enjoys visiting with friends and connecting with her family back home in Los Angeles, California.

Engineering World Health: Engineering World Health was formed to harness the resources of collegiate engineering programs for the improvement of healthcare around the world. The Purdue chapter focuses on the design of low-cost medical devices for use in developing countries.

Megan Street: Megan is an anthropology major at the University of South Dakota. She is the president of Anthropology Program Enthusiasts Society (APES). Her goals are to work in urban archaeology and to be a life-long advocate against inequality.

Allison Kim Huynh: Allison is a sophomore at the University of Texas, Austin studying neuroscience. With a passion for non-profit work, Allison has spent time in Vietnam with orphanages and schools and plans to work with Doctors Without Borders. She hopes to share with you her recent non-profit endeavor, Caring For Camo.

Kylie Johnson: Kylie is a student at the University of South Dakota. Her passion for suicide awareness and prevention started in high school and she is the current chapter president of Lost and Found at USD. Starting a conversation about suicide is her goal and she is excited to discuss the importance of it within this series.

Josie Galles and Krayton Schnepf: Josie and Krayton are both freshmen at the University of South Dakota. They teamed up and started a new organization called Then Feed Just One (TFJO). TFJO is dedicated to helping alleviate world hunger and educate others on the poverty and sufferings of third world countries. Both Josie and Krayton started with TFJO as kindergarteners in elementary school and carried it all through their years as students. The meals packaged seemed truly significant when they traveled to Honduras and saw the impact first hand. This is their way of doing something for the poor when they cannot be there full time.

Kshitij Mall: Kshitij Mall, Ashwati Das, Thomas Antony, and Prakhar Sinha are students of Aerospace department at Purdue University working on various aspects of Mars missions. They formed the Mars Society Purdue Chapter to inspire, inform, and involve the community in order to build our next home on Mars. They are all originally from India.

Ben Christiansen: Ben is from Birmingham, AL, and attended Vestavia Hills High School. He is currently pursuing a degree in biological sciences at the University of Alabama and is expected to graduate in 2018.

Madison Lewis: Madison, a Virginia Beach native, is currently a Master's student at the University of North Carolina, Wilmington hoping to graduate May 2018 with her Master's of Applied Gerontology. In May of 2016, she received her Bachelor of Science in Health Service Administration with a General Business Minor. Gerontology has been a part of Madison's life since she was a teenager, caregiving for her great grandmother at the age of just 14. She has worked in Continuing Care Retirement Communities, Assisted Living Facilities, and Rehabilitation Skilled Nursing Facilities and she loves all of the different atmospheres equally.

Made in the USA
Las Vegas, NV
26 December 2020